Praise for *Tortured Artists*

"From Lenny Bruce's separation anxiety, Charles Schulz's melancholy, Joey Ramone's OCD, and Mozart's maybe-it-was-Asperger's/maybe it was Tourette's, *Tortured Artists* offers a fascinating and funny look into those mysterious gifts that create beauty yet spring from the wells of darkness. An inspiring and addictive (no pun intended) read."
—Jessica Pallington West, author, *What Would Keith Richards Do?*

"For even the most casual aesthete, *Tortured Artists* is a chillingly familiar and clarifying journey. Christopher Zara's prose is at once simple and hauntingly complex. Required reading for any creative spirit—not to mention the unfortunate souls who have to put up with us."
—Dana P. Rowe, theatrical composer,
The Witches of Eastwick, Zombie Prom, Brother Russia

"I hate the cliché of the tortured artist, but this book shows that there is truth in the stereotype. It made me think about my own pain as an artist. Who knows? Maybe I'll be in volume two."
—Casey Spooner, artist/performer

Published by
Adams Media, a division of F+W Media, Inc.
57 Littlefield Street, Avon, MA 02322. U.S.A.
www.adamsmedia.com

ISBN 10: 1-4405-3003-3
ISBN 13: 978-1-4405-3003-6
eISBN 10: 1-4405-3211-7
eISBN 13: 978-1-4405-3211-5

Printed in the United States of America.

10   9   8   7   6   5   4   3   2   1

Library of Congress Cataloging-in-Publication Data
is available from the publisher.

This publication is designed to provide accurate and authoritative information with regard to the subject matter covered. It is sold with the understanding that the publisher is not engaged in rendering legal, accounting, or other professional advice. If legal advice or other expert assistance is required, the services of a competent professional person should be sought.
    —From a *Declaration of Principles* jointly adopted by a Committee of the American Bar Association and a Committee of Publishers and Associations

The views and opinions expressed in this work are solely those of the author, who is not a medical expert and does not imply the diagnosis of any medical or mental illness in the individuals discussed herein.

Many of the designations used by manufacturers and sellers to distinguish their product are claimed as trademarks. Where those designations appear in this book and Adams Media was aware of a trademark claim, the designations have been printed with initial capital letters.

Illustrations by Robbie Lee.

This book is available at quantity discounts for bulk purchases.
For information, please call 1-800-289-0963.

Tortured Artists

From Picasso and Monroe to Warhol and Winehouse, the Twisted Secrets of the World's Most Creative Minds

Christopher Zara
Illustrations by Robbie Lee

Adamsmedia
Avon, Massachusetts

For Christina, a remarkably efficient whip cracker who kicked my ass out of bed every morning.

What more could a guy ask for in a muse?

Contents

Part II: The Art

Introduction

"Every portrait that is painted with feeling is a portrait of the artist, not of the sitter."
—Oscar Wilde

It is sometimes said that all great art comes from pain. Van Gogh painted *Starry Night* while in emotional torment; Lennon and McCartney forged their creative partnership following the death of their respective mothers; Milton penned *Paradise Lost* after losing his wife, his daughter, and his eyesight. Such unremitting grief would send even the most grounded among us into a frenzied Xanax binge and associated fetal position, but these celebrated artists chose not to recoil in passive suffering. Instead, they turned their sorrow into something the world would cherish.

This book examines the maladies that drive creative types to the brink of despair and the inspired works that are born from their anguish. It will reveal, through the parallels hidden within the life stories of artists from all backgrounds and eras, the common thread that drives artistic expression of every conceivable sort—whether it's the magnum opus of a Renaissance master, a three-chord riff from a seventies punk band, or a keenly strewn allegory by the beloved children's book author Dr. Seuss. In the end, I'm convinced, it all starts with the same thing: a shot of intractable unpleasantness, bubbling to the surface from deep within a tortured soul.

Portrait of the Tortured Artist:
Why It's More Than a Catch Phrase

On a quiet street in Leytonstone, a remote section of East London, a six-year-old boy exits the greengrocery that bears his family name. Clutching a note that his domineering father had placed in his hand a few minutes earlier, the boy starts off toward the local police precinct a few blocks away. He stops for traffic, which in 1905 is mostly horse-drawn streetcars, then proceeds nervously to the precinct walkway.

The boy is homely by any definition. He's plump, with a round face and protruding bottom lip. His overt shortcomings are compounded by a debilitating shyness that cripples him in the presence of authority figures. Still, the boy's father gave him explicit instructions: Take the note to the station and hand it to the policeman on duty. Knowing that he had misbehaved earlier in the day, the boy is terrified that some form of punishment awaits him at his destination. Nevertheless, he carries out his father's orders. He enters the station and hands the note to the officer at the front desk. The officer reads it in silence and looks down with an impassive stare.

"Come with me," he says.

The two of them start down a long corridor and approach an empty jail cell, where the officer orders the boy to enter. With escape not an option, the boy does as he's told. He comes to the center of the cell and awaits further instructions, but before he can turn around, he hears the rumbling sound of hinge bearings rolling along the iron doorframe until the cell doors clank shut behind him. He turns to face the officer, who meets his gaze with narrowing eyes.

"This is what we do to naughty boys."

The boy watches helplessly from behind the cold, rusty bars as the officer disappears around the corridor, leaving the child alone to ponder his incarceration. Minutes pass—five, maybe six. However, they feel like hours to the boy, who spends the time wrestling with the apparent injustice of the situation. Even at this early age, he understands the concept of cruel and unusual punishment with perfect clarity. It's true he had misbehaved, but this sentence is harsh by any standard. And why was he not given a chance to defend himself? A tremor weakens the boy's knees as he is overcome by a burgeoning sense of powerlessness, until finally he is devastated by the idea that he has been forced, without cause, to surrender control to authority.

After a few more minutes, the police officer returns and unlocks the door. He smiles and pats the lad on the head, explaining how the boy's father, a personal acquaintance, had requested in the letter that his son be taught a lesson for misbehaving. However, what the boy truly learned that day went beyond a lesson in manners. He felt the helplessness of being wrongfully accused, the frustration of excessive punishment, and the complete loss of dignity that accompanies such a predicament.

Fast-forward to 1959. The boy, now pushing sixty and pudgier than ever, attends a screening of his latest film, *North by Northwest*, which he had just directed for MGM. Audiences and critics alike are riveted by the fast-paced story of a Madison Avenue ad exec, played by Cary Grant, who is mistaken for a government agent and accused of crimes he didn't commit. The film is a huge hit, and its director, Alfred Hitchcock, couldn't be more pleased.

After the screening, members of the Hollywood press, always eager to pigeonhole a person of complex talent, ask Hitchcock about his obsession with stories involving falsely accused heroes. It's a theme in Hitchcock's work that had already been well established: Richard Hannay was the target of a nationwide manhunt in *The 39 Steps*; Robert Tisdall was wrongfully accused of murder in *Young and Innocent*; and as for *The Wrong Man*, well, the title pretty much speaks for itself. Some years later, Hitchcock explains to his biographer, Charlotte Chandler, how the incident at the police precinct in Leytonstone has always stayed with him, how he never forgot the sound of the cell door clanking behind him, how a fear of incarceration and wrongful accusation has plagued him throughout his life. Many of his movies, which have come to define the suspense genre for British and American cinema, are, quite simply, an expression of that fear.

For anyone fascinated with art, and the more doleful aspects of the creative process, Alfred Hitchcock's story offers a comforting answer to a question that seems eternally elusive: "Where does art come from?" The connection between pain and art—i.e., the tortured-artist phenomenon—is probably as old as art itself. Admittedly, we have no evidence of cave painters drowning their sorrows in absinthe at trendy cafés around Paleolithic Europe, but we do know that, even then, art represented some of the most enduring hardships of society. Prehistoric paintings often depicted violent scenes of Cro-Magnon hunters being trampled by wounded animals. They were ancient obituaries, and they offer a telling window into the roots of art itself, showing pain and suffering as elementary components of the creative process.

One of the earliest written acknowledgments of the link between creativity and mental distress appears in Plato's *Phaedrus*, a dialogue in which Socrates asserts that the Muses themselves must inflict Greek poets with a "divine madness." Centuries later, Shakespeare likened his own literary vocation to insanity. "The lunatic, the lover and the poet / Are of imagination all compact," he wrote in *A Midsummer Night's Dream*.

These days, the image of the tortured artist has become something of a stereotype, whether it's Emily Dickinson condemning herself to social seclusion or Kurt Cobain bemoaning the pressures of rock stardom. But how common are these cases? Are they extreme exceptions, romanticized by a society that loves a great tragedy, or is there truth to the old cliché?

First, the science: the so-called *mad-genius phenomenon* has been studied in some scientific capacity for at least a century. Sigmund

Freud believed that creative genius came from early childhood experiences. In fact, he didn't consider creative genius a form of genius at all but rather a sign of neurosis. (To be fair, he also thought cocaine made a great antidepressant.) In more recent decades, research from various studies has revealed a measurable correlation between creativity and mental disorders, particularly bipolar disorder, which is characterized by unusually intense emotional states that occur in distinct periods of overt joy and extreme hopelessness.

The most famous of these studies was conducted in 1989 by Dr. Kay Redfield Jamison, author of the popular bipolar memoir *An Unquiet Mind*. Jamison studied forty-seven British writers and visual artists and found that 38 percent of them had been treated for a mood disorder, compared to about 7 percent of the general population. Jamison also noted that, among her subjects, the surge in creative output was often marked by an elevated mood shift, characteristic of bipolar disorder. The results led Jamison to postulate the existence of a "creativity disorder."

Does it follow, then, that we should link every last expression of human creativity to some festering hardship? Are we to see every painting in the MoMA, every movie in our Netflix queues, every song on our iPods, as the product of an antagonistic force grating on the restive psyche of some poor suffering artist? To answer yes might sound cynical, as we would all like to believe that there is, somewhere, at least *one* happy artist living among us. There isn't, of course, but then the truth that artists are universally miserable is not as bleak an interpretation as it sounds. After all, if pain and suffering are necessary ingredients for great art, then great art gives us a reason for pain and suffering. In that sense, the story of Alfred Hitchcock's prepubescent jail sentence can be consoling. It brings purpose to the unjust incarceration of a little boy and to the psychological damage it inflicted. The adult Hitchcock may have had some serious unresolved issues, but because he had issues, we have *Rear Window*, *The Birds*, and *Psycho*.

Everything humans do is the product of struggle. We invented clothes because we were cold. We built houses because we were getting rained on. We created laws because we were killing each other. You might ask why art should be any different. It's different because, even though we invented clothes, houses, and laws, we still get cold, we still get rained on, and we still kill each other. Art brings meaning to all that. It puts our pain in perspective.

Who's in This Book (and Who's Not): A Simple Explanation for Why Taylor Swift Didn't Make the Cut

According to Nielsen SoundScan, Taylor Swift is the most successful digital artist in the history of music, with 34 million songs downloaded to date. That number may induce winces from listeners who find the singer's high-gloss finish to be better suited for MOP & GLO than music, but it does raise interesting questions, such as whether or not 34 million people can really be wrong, or to what extent we can blame 34 million people for having eardrums of tin. At any rate, the reigning princess of pop-country came up while I was choosing artists for this book, largely as an exemplar of someone not to include. Mind you, this is not an excuse to pick on poor Taylor (inasmuch as someone on *Forbes* magazine's "Most Powerful Celebrities" list can be described as poor). She is, after all, an attractive, hugely famous singer, and more power to her. She also makes a lot of money, as do stockbrokers and the CEO of Chase bank. But including her in a book about genius, madness, and creativity would be like cyber winking at your cousin on OkCupid. You just know it's wrong.

For *Tortured Artists*, I chose to profile seminal creative figures from as many different disciplines and eras as possible—artists, living and dead, who not only excelled in their respective crafts but also brought something new and meaningful to them. Admittedly, picking the artists was not an exact science, but the ones who made the cut exemplify the book's title in the most quantifiable sense, which is to say they were "tortured" in a way that Johnny Cash was and "artists" in a way that Taylor Swift isn't.

WHY BEING TORTURED MATTERS

Okay, so Johnny Cash was tortured but Taylor Swift isn't. If that's true, how exactly does one measure the extent to which pain and suffering affected Johnny's art—or anyone's art, for that matter? In the 1980s, the Brown University psychiatrist Arnold Ludwig sought to answer that question with what is probably the most extensive tortured-artist study to date. Ludwig researched the lives of 1,004 prominent men and women in various fields over a period of ten years. His conclusion, as documented in his 1995 book, *The Price of Greatness*, is that people who succeed in the creative arts "suffer from more types of mental difficulties and do so over longer periods of their lives than members of the other professions."

To be fair, though, not everyone in the psychiatric community is convinced that mental anguish leads to greater artistic achievements, or even that the two are connected. Albert Rothenberg, a Harvard psychiatrist, argues in his 1990 book, *Creativity and Madness*, that the prevailing data fails to show any invariant link between the two. The data is flawed, he says, because it relies on the testimony of artists who themselves buy into the whole tortured-artist myth—folks weaned on, for instance, romantically tragic tales of van Gogh and Sylvia Plath. To further debunk the tortured-artist myth, Rothenberg cites evidence suggesting that creative people who do suffer from mood disorders are actually *more* productive when they are treated for their illnesses.

It may turn out, as Rothenberg asserts, that happy, well-adjusted people are ultimately more productive. But are they more creative?

More important, are they more artistic? The problem with scientific answers to these questions is that science tends to assume that all creative output is equal, which, let's face it, is the same as assuming that all art is equal. True, this is an absurdly subjective area, but if we can at least agree that "great" art is the art most valued by society, then the tortured-artist paradigm is bound to prevail, if only because—it bears repeating—tortured people produce better art.

One easy way to demonstrate this point is by contrasting two works by the same artist, created under different emotional circumstances. For argument's sake, let's consider the wayward career of the popular Canadian singer Alanis Morissette, who at the beginning of 1993 was approaching nineteen and already on her way to becoming a has-been. Morissette's first two albums had been studio-manufactured attempts to capitalize on the bubblegum dance craze of the late eighties, which was already a fading trend by the time the albums were released. Though she had earned the dubious distinction of being dubbed "The Debbie Gibson of Canada," Morissette did not attract much attention outside of her native country, and the albums were never released in the United States. (We already have a Debbie Gibson, thank you.)

Then the singer's personal life took a turn for the dramatic. Her record label dumped her, and, in an instant, it seemed as if her dreams of pop stardom were over. She decided to ditch her insular hometown of Ottawa, moving first to Toronto and then Los Angeles, where for the first time in her life she was on her own. She encountered strife, hardship, bad relationships. But as her life sputtered out of control, Morissette discovered something entirely new to her—namely, something interesting to write about.

And write she did, channeling the anger, pain, and heartbreak of her sputtering life into the 1995 rock album *Jagged Little Pill*. The album became a runaway sensation, spending more than a year on the U.S. *Billboard* 200. Its gutsy, unapologetic lyrics inspired a new generation of female rock singers, and Morissette went from being compared to Debbie Gibson to being christened a modern-day Janis Joplin. Unfortunately, Morissette's newfound status as a revered musical phenom came with a downside. With enormous success and adoration, the angry, embittered singer found herself significantly less angry and bitter. The change was great for her personal life but not so great for her efforts to write new music. Three years later, her long-awaited follow-up to *Jagged Little Pill*, the clumsily titled *Supposed Former Infatuation Junkie*, enjoyed a strong debut, but then it dropped quickly from the charts, with sales of less than 20 percent of its predecessor's. Critics and fans were not oblivious to the abrupt shift in Morissette's lyrics, which had traded anger and aggression for contentment and serenity. Suddenly, the jilted vixen who scratched her nails down some guy's back out of spite for an ex-lover was making spiritual pilgrimages to India, and the result failed to resonate with audiences. When Morissette lost her pain, her art lost its way, and audiences noticed. That change, in a nutshell, signifies the role of pain in the creative process.

THAT'S GREAT, BUT WHAT IS ART?

Because critics, philosophers, and other intellectual beard strokers argue over the definition of art, we often make the mistake of assuming that its definition must be complex. Richard Wollheim, the late philosopher of aesthetics, has said that trying to define the nature of art is "one of the most elusive of the traditional problems of human culture." And yet we never seem to have a difficult time defining art for ourselves. Mark Rothko's Abstract Expressionist painting *No. 5/No. 22* is hanging in New York's Museum of Modern Art for one reason: Someone thought it was art. You or I may happen to think it looks like a swath of Russian salad dressing, but then we're not the curators of MoMA.

For *Tortured Artists*, I was more concerned with whether something could be considered art in the categorical sense. Is its primary purpose an aesthetic one? If not, I couldn't include it. This means that the book does not feature profiles of, for instance, architects, who employ a great deal of artistry in their work but who ultimately create utilitarian structures for which aesthetic considerations are secondary. Buildings can be beautiful, but they're not art. And with all due respect to all those mean reality-show chefs, food is not art either.

Admittedly, the line between artist and artisan is not always clear. Alexander McQueen, the tortured fashion designer who in 2010 hanged himself with his "favorite brown belt," often created costumes whose only purpose was aesthetic in nature. He would have made a fascinating profile, but I had to make a judgment call not to include fashion designers.

Ultimately, I wanted *Tortured Artists* to comprise the broadest sampling of eras and artistic genres possible, without telling the same repetitive stories about poor alcoholics whose mothers never loved them. Of course, this is not a complete list. Arthur Rimbaud, Jimi Hendrix, Spalding Gray—although these artists are mentioned in the Tortured Artists Timeline at the back of this book, I would have liked to include full profiles on each of them, not to mention countless others. Naturally, space prohibits a profile on every influential tortured artist who has ever lived, but if choosing Sylvia Plath over Virginia Woolf seems arbitrary, that's because it is, at least partially. Taste is a highly idiosyncratic sense, after all. How else can we account for the tremendous but logic-defying popularity of Taylor Swift? Poor, rich Taylor Swift.

PART I

The Demons

1

The First Twelve Years

Death, Disease, Abuse, Neglect, and Other Sordid Tales of Prepubescence

Childhood trauma increases our risk for pretty much every affliction on the planet. It is the launching point for all the things that can go wrong with our bodies, our minds, our lives. The scientific explanation for this is simple: Early stressors lead to emotional problems, which lead to risky behaviors, which lead to diseases or accidents, which lead to death. And yet, ironically, the creative world owes a great debt to childhood trauma, which can plant the seeds for brilliant artistic achievements. Imagine, for instance, how Josephine Baker's life might

Josephine Baker

have been different had she not witnessed the race riot of East St. Louis, in 1917. At the age of ten, the future "Bronze Venus" of the Ziegfeld Follies was ripped from her bed by her mother, who pulled her to safety as the city exploded in flames and African Americans were hunted down and clubbed in the streets before her eyes. Would Baker, without this experience, have fled the United States for France? Would she have gone on to become the first African-American female to achieve international stardom?

To cite another example, the country singer Patsy Cline had a serious throat infection as a child. Although the disease nearly killed her, Cline later boasted to reporters that she recovered from the infection sounding like Kate Smith, the golden-voiced singer who popularized the song "God Bless America." Most of us view childhood afflictions as tragic, and they are. However, artists like Baker, Cline, and the ones covered in this chapter prove that a good childhood trauma doesn't have to go to waste.

These are the tales of how some of the world's most tortured artists first became tortured.

Pablo Picasso
(1881–1973)

Abstract: A million little pieces
Birth name: Pablo Ruiz y Picasso
Birthplace: Malaga, Spain
Masterwork: *Guernica*
Demons: Devastation and restoration

"With me, a picture is a sum of destructions."
—**Interview with the art critic Christian Zervos, 1934**

Perhaps the easiest way to gauge the illustriousness of any historical figure is by putting his or her last name through the insult test. The more famous the name, the more effectively it doubles as an insult when coupled with a negative adjective. Hence the math challenged among us are said to be "no Einsteins," the poor are "no Rockefellers," and if your charcoal sketch of a nude woman looks like something out of the *Orphanet Journal of Rare Diseases*, you will probably be told that you are "no Picasso." The ironic bite of such insults resides in knowing how impossibly high their eponyms set the bar. A lousy artist may be no Picasso, but then who is? The foremost painter of the twentieth century has one of those names that far outstrip the medium for which they are known.

Rebelliousness, innovation, obsession—for each of these notably Picasso-esque qualities, the artist could thank his father, José Ruiz y

Blasco, an art teacher and museum curator. It was José, first and foremost, who recognized Pablo's extraordinary artistic talent and gave him the training to capitalize on it. Truth be told, it was even José from whom Picasso inherited his famously overactive libido. (José was an avowed bachelor until the age of forty, which doesn't sound like much until you consider that life expectancy at the time was only forty-two.) When Pablo was seventeen, José handed his paints and brushes to his son and swore off painting for good. Pablo was the genius of the family; that much was clear. In fact, the only thing outpacing Pablo's talent was his ego, and, before long, the obstinate young artist abandoned all that his father valued in art, including the idea that an artist should be formally trained. However, obstinacy alone does not make a creative pioneer, and had it not been for one horrific incident in Pablo's early childhood—years before his artistic gifts surfaced—he may have never emerged as the watershed figure of modern art.

"the only thing outpacing Pablo's talent was his ego"

On Christmas Day, 1884, the Great Andalusian Earthquake rocked southern Spain, killing as many as 900 people and destroying more than 14,000 houses and buildings. Among those caught in its wake were a three-year-old Pablo and his family, who took refuge in a cave as the city of Malaga crumbled to pieces around them. The trembling ground induced Pablo's pregnant mother into labor, and the toddler watched with his mouth agape as she gave birth to his younger sister. Though the adult Pablo rarely spoke of the earthquake that almost ended his life, its influence on his psyche became evident years later when the concept of a broken reality emerged as the hallmark characteristic of Cubism, the revolutionary artistic movement that Picasso, along with the French painter Georges Braque, pioneered.

It doesn't take a neo-Freudian art therapist to view Picasso's most famous Cubist works as verification that the artist's inner child had become permanently fractured.

Objects in Cubist works are broken up, analyzed, and reassembled in abstract form. The technique, a bold departure from the Post-Impressionism of the era, abandons modes of perspective that had been used by artists since the Renaissance, renouncing logical space in favor of abstract representations of objects shown from multiple angles at once.

Is it a stretch to trace Picasso's visionary artistic style to an earthquake? Some experts don't think so. In her 1988 book, *The Untouched Key*, the Polish psychologist Alice Miller, who until her death in 2010 was one of the foremost experts on childhood trauma, argued that because the earthquake took place when Picasso was so young, the experience made a permanent mark on his developing mind. Even Picasso's infamous preoccupation with sex and the female body, Miller reasons, might have been the result of seeing the birth of his sister under such violent circumstances. "How does a woman giving birth look to a three-year-old boy," Miller asks, "and what happens in the young boy's psyche when the woman writhing in pain happens to be his mother?"

To be sure, Picasso's fate as a successful artist was sealed early in his life. But before he had displayed any prodigious gifts, before he rebelled against his father, before his hormones kicked in, he learned, in one fleeting instant, that reality is easily breakable and difficult to restore. It's interesting to ponder what path he would have taken had the earthquake not shaken his world at such an impressionable age. Given his natural talents, it's safe to say that Picasso would still have enjoyed a very pleasant career in art. But then he would have been no Picasso. ⌁

Clara Bow
(1905–1965)

Abstract: The star who almost wasn't born
Birth name: Clara Gordon Bow
Birthplace: Brooklyn, New York, USA
Peak performance: As Betty Lou Spence in *It*, 1927
Demons: Abuse, neglect, indigence, more abuse

"No one wanted me to be born in the first place."
—Interview with *Motion Picture Classic* magazine, 1928

In February 1927, eight short months before minstrel Al Jolson sang "My Mammy" to enthralled moviegoers who had never before heard pictures talk, the ill-fated silent movie industry had itself one last fling: Paramount Pictures' romantic comedy *It*, about a flirtatious flapper who develops a crush on her wealthy playboy of a boss, became a runaway box-office hit thanks to the uncompromising sex appeal of its twenty-one-year-old leading lady, Clara Bow. For a medium that required no dialogue, Clara had the perfect tools. Her giant black eyes were as expressive as they were haunted, and her beguiling flits of exuberance could evoke lustful tingles from an audience of asexual spores. She had no formal acting training but could wow directors by laughing hysterically one minute and crying on cue the next. In this fledgling art form called *motion pictures*, which was less than three decades old and still highly self-conscious, Clara introduced something entirely original: a complete lack of onscreen inhibition. Dubbed the "It" girl, she quickly became a national sensation, personifying the new, sexually liberated woman of the Roaring Twenties. F. Scott Fitzgerald called her "the quintessence of what the term 'flapper' signifies . . . pretty, impudent, superbly assured." By the spring of 1927, young girls across the country were emulating this brash gadabout who smoked in public, drank gin, flirted openly, cursed, and listened to jazz.

"young girls across the country were emulating this brash gadabout who smoked in public, drank gin, flirted openly, cursed, and listened to jazz"

There were other flapper-era starlets, of course—Louise Brooks, Greta Garbo—but they were poseurs by comparison. Unlike Brooks, who was from rural Kansas, and Garbo, a Swedish immigrant, Clara was a true Jazz Baby, raised in the slums of Brooklyn by an alcoholic father who neglected her and a mentally ill mother who once tried to slice her open with a butcher knife. From the very beginning, she was unwanted and underestimated: Born in July 1905, during a record heat wave that pushed the infant mortality rate to 80 percent, Clara was not expected to survive birth, and in fact her parents never bothered to obtain a birth certificate.

Her earliest years were spent in a poverty-stricken tenement neighborhood where epidemics of smallpox and cholera were the norm and ill-kempt drains filled the hallways with human waste.

When Clara was three, her grandfather, the only relative who had ever shown her any affection, died of a heart attack while pushing her on a swing, prompting her mother to coldly remark to the toddler, "Clara,

I wish it had been you." Clara's father, a trollish ne'er-do-well who spent most of his time in brothels and saloons, would disappear for days and weeks at a stretch, leaving Clara and her mother to fend for themselves.

On days when Clara's father was home, he was either ignoring Clara completely or rapping her across the face with his leather razor strop. At school, Clara was tormented by classmates who mimicked her stutter and ridiculed her homemade clothes, which were usually fashioned out of her mother's old shirtwaists. It was a dreary childhood, a nightmare of Cinderellic proportions, but as Clara once said in an interview, there was at least one place she could go to escape it all: "That was to the motion pictures. I can never repay them what they gave me."

In an age when we spend every waking hour with our eyeballs glued to computer screens, smart phones, Kindles, iPads, and televisions, it's easy to forget that there was a time, not so long ago, when none of these things existed. Clara Bow, born at the dawn of the twentieth century, belonged to a unique cohort—the first to grow up watching moving images on a screen. Accordingly, she and her peers were the first to have their minds molded by the subversive ideals of a hilly West Coast district known as Hollywood. As movies took their place atop the entertainment totem pole, their larger-than-life allure gave rise to a new breed of fame-chasing American youth, one that coveted the adoration showered upon the likes of Mary Pickford and Wallace Reid. To the ignored, unloved young Clara, hiding from the world in a dark movie house, such adoration seemed as though it would validate her very existence. All she needed was a break, which came at the age of sixteen when her portrait won the annual "Fame and Fortune" photo contest run by Brewster Publications. Clara, despite the fact that she had never performed on camera, naively hoped to parlay the modest accolade into a full-time movie career.

Her lack of experience turned out to be a blessing in disguise. Whereas other stars of the early screen were victims of their own expertise—theater-bred thespians determined to "act" for the camera lens—Clara knew only how to be herself. Her performances were impulsive and erratic but never contrived. Like the title of her hit film suggested, Clara had "It," the elusive quality that separates stars from the rest of us. Her intense natural spark helped define a broad new spectrum of femininity—the flirt, the life of the party, the Hollywood sex symbol—but all of these exhibitionist personas were driven by the same unquenchable need for attention and love, two things she never knew in childhood.

After *It*, Clara became one of the top box-office draws in Hollywood, but her popularity was short lived. On October 6, 1927, Warner Bros. released *The Jazz Singer*, the first sound-synched feature film, prompting a technological shift of unprecedented speed and unstoppable force. Within two years, nearly every studio release was a talkie. Clara Bow, like Chaplin, Valentino, and scores of other silent stars, did not successfully make the transition to sound. Her millions of adoring fans had yet to hear her speak, and when she finally did, she sounded more like a sailor than a starlet, spewing a profanity-laced, G-dropping Brooklynese that no amount of dialect coaching could correct. Clara's cultural cache soon gave way to Betty Boop, the iconic cartoon flapper created partly in her image by animator Grim Natwick. Overnight, the vivacious young actress became a caricature, a relic of the previous decade, whose hard-partying socialite image seemed frivolous and out of touch amid the ensuing years of the Great Depression. In 1933, disgusted and discouraged after a string of commercial failures, Clara quit the film business forever. She was twenty-six. ~

Cel Damage

In 1930, Fleischer Studios premiered *Dizzy Dishes*, the first cartoon to feature Betty Boop, a character modeled after Clara Bow. While Clara's thick Brooklyn accent thwarted the actress's attempt to transition to sound films, that same trait ironically became one of Betty's most endearing trademarks. A few years later, however, in what might be described as a bit of cartoon karma, Betty suffered the same fate as Clara, failing to transition successfully into color cartoons.

Johnny Cash
(1932–2003)

Abstract: Black on the inside
Birth name: J. R. Cash
Birthplace: Kingsland, Arkansas, USA
Masterworks: "I Walk the Line," "Ring of Fire"
Demons: Guilt

"There's no way around grief and loss. You can dodge all you want, but sooner or later you just have to go into it, through it, and, hopefully, come out the other side."
—From *Johnny Cash: The Autobiography,* 1998

Anyone who grew up north of the Mason-Dixon Line has heard the phrase "I hate country music." What's interesting, though, is how often we unapologetic Yankees qualify that declaration with the addendum, "but I love me some Johnny Cash." And why wouldn't we? The brooding, black-clad singer bridged a stark divide that emerged in the recording industry in the 1950s, as post-Elvis pop singers diverged into two camps and audiences aligned themselves with either the sideburned rebels of rock 'n' roll or the cowboy-hatted twangsters of country music. Cash, if nothing else, proved that the latter genre is not just for beer-bellied good ole boys who adorn their Ford pickup trucks with busty-girl mud flaps. Everyone, from politicians to pole dancers, can appreciate Johnny Cash (no less than five U.S. presidents have declared themselves fans of the singer), and it's not just because he looked cool in black and had a baritone voice that could cut through raw iron. Cash endures because his most well-known songs—"I Walk the Line" and "Ring of Fire" among them—weave deeply personal narratives with which listeners of all stripes can effortlessly identify. In short, the guy knew how to tell a good story, a skill he may have never discovered had it not been for what is probably the most singularly traumatic childhood event out of any in this chapter.

Imagine going through life feeling responsible for the death of your own brother. Such was the deeply felt—though unearned— guilt that served as the framing device for Johnny Cash's perpetually black core. His brother's death occurred just as Johnny was crossing the delicate threshold from preteen to manhood. At that time, he still went by his legal birth name, J. R., so christened because his parents, apparently, could not agree on what to call him.

One morning in May 1944, when J. R. was twelve, he set out to go fishing while his older brother Jack prepared for work at the high school agriculture shop where he had a job cutting timber. The job paid only $3 a day, but the fourteen-year-old Jack felt a strong sense of responsibility to help provide for the struggling Cash family, which included his parents, who picked cotton for a living, and six brothers and sisters. But something did not seem right on that Saturday morning. Both J. R. and Jack were overcome by a lingering sense that tragedy awaited Jack at the wood shop. It was one of those eerie premonitions that, after the fact, leave us wondering why we didn't just trust our gut instincts. Indeed, J. R. did urge Jack to trust that gut instinct, begging his older brother to blow off work and go fishing with him instead, but Jack, a dutiful lad to a fault, opted for the more responsible choice.

Later that day, the boys' premonition came to harrowing fruition. Jack, who was apparently working without adult supervision, lost his balance while trying to cut a board. He fell onto a giant head saw, whose whirling, jagged blade sliced him almost in half, creating a gash from his ribcage, down through his stomach, all the way to his groin. The boy did not die instantly, however. Instead, he suffered for several days in a hospital bed, and at one point even showed signs that he might actually get bet-

"the future country-music legend never shook off the feeling that he could have somehow prevented the tragedy"

ter, despite his doctor's insistence that a full recovery was impossible. "I had to take out too many of his insides," the physician told the boy's parents. Jack succumbed to his injuries the next day. As for J. R., the future country-music legend never shook off the feeling that he could have somehow prevented the tragedy.

J. R.'s feeling of guilt was exacerbated by his father, Ray, who often bluntly pointed out the irony that the hardworking Jack was killed while J. R., the good-for-nothing layabout who chose fishing over work, lived on. Ray Cash was not exactly an even-tempered sort to begin with (he once shot the family dog because it ate too many table scraps), but Jack's death opened up a channel through which the hardened old man expressed his favoritism more viciously than ever. Like Clara Bow's mother decades earlier, Ray Cash made his callous druthers entirely clear, telling J. R. flatly that it should have been he, not Jack, who died on that fateful day. Even the most stoic among us would be wounded by that, but J. R., a Baptist for whom guilt was written into his DNA, carried the burden of his brother's death for the rest of his days.

"[He] had this real sad guilt thing about him his whole life," Cash's daughter Kathy once said of her father. "You could see it in his eyes. You can look at almost any picture and see this dark, sadness thing going on."

In the months following Jack's death, the young J. R. became obsessively fixated on the incident. In the summer of 1944, he went to Boy Scout camp and talked of nothing but Jack; however, somewhere between pitching tents and learning how to tie square knots, J. R.'s fellow scouts grew tired of hearing him drone on about his dead brother. Eventually they told him it was time to give it a rest. "I got the message," Cash said. "I quit talking about Jack altogether. Everybody knew how I felt and how my mother felt; they didn't need us telling them."

Cash rarely spoke of the tragedy after that, but then it's not the kind of thing one shrugs off either. Instead, the grieving boy entered puberty in an endless pursuit of escapist reveries, losing himself in radio dramas, westerns, and oral tales of the Old Frontier told by the various vagabonds who passed through his small Arkansas town. These seemingly pedestrian pastimes taught J. R. something invaluable about the art of storytelling. He learned that stories have to have purpose, a core, something for people to grab onto. Aimless blathering, he soon realized, does not appeal to listeners' sympathies, even if it concerns something as profound as a brother's death. J. R.'s informal education in storytelling equipped him with skills to craft sharp, accessible narratives, a talent he used when later writing the songs that would bring him worldwide acclaim. From his first commercial hit, "Cry, Cry, Cry," in which the protagonist laments the trysts of his unfaithful lover, to the folk-inspired "Folsom Prison Blues," in which a convict listens longingly to the sounds of the outside world, Cash's songs gave a crisp structure to willfully somber topics.

The day Jack Cash died was the day the sad, soulful, brooding Johnny Cash was born. It created the heaviness of spirit that transformed him into the original Man in Black—a country star whose dark wardrobe was less a style choice than the reflection of a perpetually dark inner being. ～

Andy Warhol
(1928–1987)

Abstract: The unsightly celebrity apprentice
Birth name: Andrew Warhola Jr.
Birthplace: Pittsburgh, Pennsylvania, USA
Masterworks: *Campbell's Soup Cans, Brillo Boxes*
Demons: Disease and self-hatred

"I usually accept people on the basis of their self-images, because their self-images have more to do with the way they think than their objective-images do."
—From *The Philosophy of Andy Warhol*, 1975

You have to hand it to Andy Warhol. For a silly-looking guy reminiscent of Gollum in a mad-scientist wig, he had, and still has, the ability to ruffle feathers among folks who take art seriously. The seminal pop artist was an interesting character, no doubt, but was he a true artist? Such is the question that has occupied critics, aesthetes, and pretty much anyone who has an opinion about art since Warhol first surfaced in the 1950s.

Long before Andy emerged as the timid oddity of New York City counterculture, he was the timid oddity of Holmes Elementary School in Depression-era Pittsburgh. From his earliest interactions with his peers, Andrew Warhola, the son of Slovakian immigrants, was beset by hypersensitivity—a kid for whom socializing was an ordeal of the most terrifying variety. On his first day of kindergarten, he got slapped in the face by a little girl and, through tears, vowed to his mother that he would never return to school again.

But it was in 1936, when Andy entered the third grade, that he went from mere oddity to object of ridicule. His life was upended that year by a serious bout with chorea, a neurological condition thought to be a complication of scarlet fever. Undiagnosed at first, the disease **"the experiences pushed him further and further into isolation"** covered him with reddish-brown blotches on his face, back, chest, arms, and hands. It also caused thinning hair and involuntary muscle movements. The eight-year-old Andy was tormented by his classmates, who would mock his shaking hands when he tried to write on the blackboard. The experiences pushed him further and further into isolation until finally, after a doctor identified the condition, his mother took him out of school altogether.

If ever there had been any question of Andy's role as the delicate flower of the Warhola family, his disease put such doubts to rest. Far more squeamish than his two older brothers, Andy had long proven himself the sensitive one, the one who needed special care, and his mother, Julia, had gotten into the habit of coddling him to the extreme. But now, in his ailing state, Andy was at the mercy of this overprotective woman. Though well intentioned, Julia was a chronic doter, a maternal force of Pink Floydian scope, and her smothering presence inadvertently squeezed out any ounce of self-esteem he had left. "She made him feel insignificant," a friend of Andy's later noted. "She made him feel that he was the ugliest creature that God put on this earth."

It was during this low period in Andy's life, a time when he felt the most helpless and hideous, that the future Prince of Pop Art began to develop an intense fascination with beauty and celebrity, a fascination that would define him as an artist.

Bedridden for several weeks, he escaped into the fantasy world of movie magazines and the glamorous culture of 1930s screen stars. He lost himself in glossy photographs of Joan Crawford, Bette Davis, Marlene Dietrich; their beauty and poise, their airbrushed perfection, represented everything he was not. He steadied his hand tremors long enough to cut out the photos and make collages of his favorite stars. This was the world Andy dreamed of joining, and yet he already sensed that it was an elite club to which he could never really belong.

As Andy plodded through adolescence and into young adulthood, the blotches on his skin slowly began to fade, mostly clearing up by the time he graduated from the Carnegie Institute of Technology in 1949. His first taste of professional success came in the 1950s, in New York City, where he found work as a commercial illustrator for magazines and ad agencies. However, it was as a fine artist, in the 1960s, that Andy began to attract the attention of the art world with his silkscreen paintings of celebrities and household products. The images, smooth and machinelike in appearance, stood in proud contrast to the stringy and cluttered Abstract Expressionism that dominated New York's art scene at the time. Pollock's and de Kooning's canvas-abusing tactics, with their gestural brushstrokes and antifigurative compositions, felt like old hat next to Andy's fetish for mass-produced iconography, which challenged the very idea of what fine art could be.

However, if success as an artist validated Andy's creative ambitions, it did little to quell his negative self-image. As an invalid, he had learned what it meant to be the thing society values least—a disposable human being. But as a pop artist, he would force society to rethink the value of things it once deemed disposable: Campbell's

Soup cans, Brillo boxes, Coca-Cola bottles. His desire to give these objects equal face time with Marilyn, Elvis, and Liz Taylor sprung from a futile longing to be one of the beautiful people. Nevertheless, he remained determined, throughout his career, to dissolve the barriers between beauty and ugliness, and in the process he blurred the line between art and commerce.

There is still, of course, the matter of Warhol's endless detractors, who insist that the man was nothing more than a champion of consumerism cloaked in pseudo-avant-gardery. To them, Andy's nonchalant oddness opened the floodgates for a "do it because it's weird" philosophy that still haunts the art world in the form of elephant dung, silent raves, and boxes of rocks. Admittedly, it's hard to argue that a rough childhood is an acceptable excuse for making people sit through a five-hour movie about some guy sleeping, but then Warhol's critics still miss an important point. Anyone can censure artistic pretense from behind *The New York Times'* Arts & Leisure section, but only Andy Warhol, who had come face-to-face with his own grotesqueness, could have mocked that world from within its own pretentious circles, and decades after the fact, it's easy to see that he was in on the joke. After looking at his work, one might very well come to the conclusion that a painting of a Coke bottle is no more a work of art than the syrupy drink it represents, but we're at least forced to think about it. To Andy, that was the point. "A Coke is a Coke," he once wrote. "No amount of money can get you a better Coke than the one the bum on the corner is drinking. All the Cokes are the same, and all the Cokes are good." ⟿

Michael Jackson
(1958–2009)

Abstract: The good son goes bad
Birth name: Michael Joseph Jackson
Birthplace: Gary, Indiana, USA
Masterwork: *Thriller*
Demons: Name it.

"I don't know if I was his golden child or whatever, but he was very strict, very hard, very stern. Just a look would scare you."
—Speaking about his father in an interview with Oprah Winfrey, 1993

Michael Jackson was a true American tragedy. Swept up by a tornado of attention in early childhood, the pop singer skyrocketed to the top of the entertainment food chain only to descend like a uni-gloved fallen angel into tabloid freakdom. And yet he was a monster of our own making, a Frankenstein's creature spawned by a fickle American public that is eager to grant celebrity status and even more eager to kick the pedestal out from under those upon whom celebrity status has been bestowed. Jackson's life has always been viewed under a dual lens: part microscope, part kaleidoscope. But ever since his death from propofol intoxication in 2009, it has become all but impossible to distinguish between the different personages of the

Jacksonian Trinity. The man, the myth, the monster—they are one and the same now. Jackson may have defined the sound and style of a generation, but the peculiarities of his existence will forever footnote his achievements.

True, he is among the most recognizable entertainers in history, but he also hung out with a chimpanzee, dangled his son over a balcony, and shared a bed with Macaulay Culkin. Further tarnishing his legacy are the multiple claims by parents that he sexually abused their children. Add it all up and you have a downright maddening composite of artistry, criminality, and legend.

Few people will argue that Michael Jackson was not a quintessential example of a tortured artist. The problem is that determining what tortured him can be an overwhelming, kid-in-a-candy-store experience for anyone who seeks to unearth such things. Pick a personal demon, and chances are Jackson was tortured by it. He grew up dirt poor, one of nine brothers and sisters who lived shoulder-to-shoulder in a two-bedroom hovel. He spent his childhood in constant fear of Joe Jackson, the tyrannical father who, whip in hand, pushed Michael and his brothers into show business. He went through his awkward stage in front of the entire world, singing and dancing like a trained seal as the reluctant front-boy of the phenomenally successful group the Jackson Five. Later he became plagued by an unyielding perfectionism that, combined with a self-hating streak, resulted in endless plastic surgeries. And, of course, underlying all of these issues was the question of his sexual orientation, if we are to believe he even had one.

But none of Jackson's demons would have meant a thing if it weren't for the astounding effect he had on pop music as a solo artist—a feat that has solidified his permanence as a central figure of the 1980s. When aliens land on Earth and ask us to sum up the decade, all we will need to do is whip out the iconic 1984 photograph of Jackson flanked by the Reagans in front of the South Portico of the White House.

Jackson's era-defining presence is unmatched, and for that he can thank his single most salient personal demon: his desire to break free from the insurmountable control of his dictatorial father. Not much about Joe Jackson will come as a shock. He is essentially a broad caricature of the American showbiz parent: controlling, abusive, shamelessly exploitive. Once an aspiring rhythm-and-blues musician himself, he abandoned those dreams to raise a family. But when he discovered that the family he was raising, particularly Michael, had inherited his musical gifts, he saw a vicarious opportunity. He also saw a meal ticket, a way to escape the steel mills of Indiana in which he worked as a crane operator.

Early rehearsals for the Jackson Five were like boot camp. Joe would watch with a belt in his hands, making sure the children performed as they should. "You could not mess up," Michael said. "If you didn't do it the right way, he would tear you up, really get you."

Joe's abuse was not just physical, nor did it end when the Jackson Five found success

"further tarnishing his legacy are the multiple claims by parents that he sexually abused their children"

in the early 1970s. When Michael hit puberty, his father, like a festering canker sore, was right there to aggravate his growing pains. Just as the group's popularity was beginning to wane, Michael's self-hating tendencies kicked into full gear. He looked in the mirror and saw kinky hair and a shovel-shaped nose at a time when other young stars of the era looked like Keith Partridge. Indeed, the tabloid rumor that Michael once sought to purchase the bones of the Elephant Man was at least grounded in a truth that the singer felt a kinship with the disfigured Englishman Joseph Merrick. ("He reminds me of me a lot.") Joe Jackson didn't help matters, calling his son ugly and teasing him when his skin broke out in acne—all as a means to keep Michael under his control.

When Michael was twenty years old, however, something happened that would help him finally free himself: He teamed up with the producer Quincy Jones. The two first worked together on the set of the 1978 film version of *The Wiz*. The film was a critical and financial flop, but Jones, who adapted it from its original stage version, saw in Michael something that Joe Jackson apparently never bothered to look for: potential as a creative artist. Joe never had a problem exploiting his son's immense talent, but allowing Michael creative control had always been out of the question.

Quincy Jones felt the opposite way. Upon working with Michael the first time, he believed, instantly, that deep within this trained seal lurked a creative genius. "It was that wonderment that I saw in his eyes that locked me in," he once said. "I knew that we could go into completely unexplored territory." Jones thought so highly of Michael's potential that when the singer asked him to recommend a producer, Jones volunteered. Michael, who saw in Jones the encouraging father figure he never had, agreed to let him take the reins.

The result was the 1979 album *Off the Wall*, a palatable combination of disco, jazz, soft ballads, and synth-pop. The album was a runaway success, the first in history to produce more than three top-ten singles on the *Billboard* charts. It heralded not only the rebirth of Michael Jackson as an artist but also the birth of the 1980s. And yet there was even more to come. As big as *Off the Wall* was, it would ultimately pale in comparison to Michael and Jones's second collaboration. *Thriller*, released in 1982, became one of the defining soundtracks of the decade and remains to this day the bestselling album of all time.

Unfortunately, Michael's surrogate father–son bond with Jones was not enough to undo the abuse inflicted by Joe Jackson. The years of regimented rehearsals and fear of being reprimanded saddled him with a perfectionist attitude that he would never shake. Watch footage of his performances: Every note, every dance step, is calculated with nuanced precision. But it was the combination of that precision coupled with the creative freedom granted by Quincy Jones that ignited the worldwide pop explosion he became. And what of Michael's tragic third act—the tabloid "wacko" and bizarre sideshow? Considering his one-time mythic celebrity status, such an outcome was probably inevitable. Nature has a way of balancing things out. Consequently, Michael's legacy will always be dubious, caught in a tug of war between national treasure and American tragedy. ∽

Wolfgang Amadeus Mozart
(1756–1791)

Abstract: The first case against child stardom
Birth name: Johannes Chrysostomus Wolfgangus Theophilus Mozart
Birthplace: Salzburg, Austria
Masterwork: *The Abduction from the Seraglio*
Demons: Impossible expectations

"It is a mistake to think that the practice of my art has become easy to me."
—A remark to Conductor Kucharz, Prague, 1787

What the hell was wrong with Mozart? Few questions in the vast canons of tortured-artist scholarship have produced more theories than this one. According to the *British Medical Journal*, the psychiatric community has, over the years, ascribed to the composer no less than twenty-seven distinct mental illnesses. For instance, his tremendous creative output was the result of manic-depressive disorder; his poor people skills, Asperger's syndrome; his fondness for scatological humor, a sign of Tourette's. You get the idea. It's as if an official diagnosis is the only way to account for his extraordinary abilities.

And extraordinary they were.

Mozart was composing and sight-reading music at an age when most of us are still trying to master the sippy cup. As an adult, he could work out entire symphonies in his head and transcribe them to paper without making a single error, sometimes while playing billiards on the side.

However, the damaging psychological impact of his music career was not so different from that of any number of former child stars whose glazed mug shots sometimes show up on *Gawker*. The highs and lows of Mozart's life resulted from the forced immersion into show business and celebrity culture. Sound familiar? Adjust the circumstances for eighteenth-century Austria, and Wolfgang starts to look a lot like Michael Jackson in a puffy shirt. Indeed, the lives of these two precocious music artists were so eerily similar that one wonders if Wolfgang did not somehow successfully lobby for reincarnation.

In the preceding profile, we saw how Joe Jackson, Michael's dictatorial father, left no opportunistic stone unturned as he exploited his young son's musical talents, hoping to elevate the Jackson family from their humble Indiana roots. Similarly, Mozart's own father, Leopold, was keen on profiting from his son's gifts as soon as they began to surface. He wasted no time in parading his toddler around the royal courts of Munich, Vienna,

"the psychiatric community has, over the years, ascribed to the composer no less than twenty-seven distinct mental illnesses"

and Prague, astonishing throngs of aristocrats with Wolfgang's ability to play impeccable pieces of music with his doll-sized hands. Leopold, a washed-up composer by the time Wolfgang was born, knew the potential value of his son's talent and was eager to abandon his work as a teacher to assume the role of master showman, touting the abilities of his son with ringmaster-like flare. According to Leopold's own description, raw genius like Wolfgang's "probably comes to light but once in a century."

That all of this profiteering and exploitation might be considered poor parenting is not an idea unique to modern times. Just as Joe Jackson has received much criticism for denying Michael a normal childhood in exchange for child stardom, Leopold Mozart got his share of flack for cash-cowifying young Wolfgang. To his critics, Leopold would assert his convenient belief that Wolfgang's talent was a gift from God and so he had a divine duty to share that gift with the world. Wolfgang, like any child star who is thrust into the limelight, learned to crave praise like a drug—with unchecked vanity as a side effect.

However, his vanity turned on him after a serious case of smallpox disfigured his face with pitted scars. (He was eleven at the time and already extremely fussy about his appearance.) His self-loathing became more severe as he grew older but not taller. The fact that he barely topped five feet always humiliated him, as did his large nose, which he surely would have butchered, Jackson-style, had plastic surgery been a viable option.

As an adult, Wolfgang, like Michael, came to a moment when he finally resolved to break free of his oppressive father. That ultimate act of rebellion led him to ditch his native Salzburg, in 1781, and carve out a career for himself in Vienna, where he experienced an astounding creative awakening. The following year, he composed the German Singspiel opera *The Abduction from the Seraglio*, commissioned by the Austrian Emperor Joseph II. The opera was heralded throughout the German-speaking world as a groundbreaking achievement. Goethe, Germany's most prominent author at the time, said it "knocked everything else sideways." It was Mozart's *Thriller*, a veritable pop-music phenomenon that signified his transition from prodigal parlor trick to gifted composer.

Which brings us back to the question of what the hell was wrong with Mozart. The answer is perhaps more prosaic than his genius deserves. His life certainly panned out in a way consistent with child-star tragedies of today. After achieving early success, he spent his thirties plagued by financial problems, difficulty in finding work, and ill health. Mozart lived his final years in a state of constant depression, his ego shattered by his diminishing fame. The illness that caused his death at the age of thirty-five remains a mystery, although the medical community has offered more than its fair share of possible diagnoses (140 at last count). In the end, however, Mozart was not a tortured prodigy who happened to become a child star, but a tortured child star who happened to be a prodigy. ～

Aural Apocalypse

Mozart's uncanny musical gift was not without its shortcomings. In fact, the same razor-sharp sense of sound that allowed him to pinpoint musical notes with impeccable precision also plagued him with hypersensitive hearing. As a young boy, his growing ears were so delicate that he could not bear the shrilly sound of a trumpet solo until he reached the age of ten. In 1766, the renowned Swiss neurologist Samuel Tissot even wrote an article about the boy Mozart's sensitivity, noting that "wrong, harsh, or excessively loud sounds" often brought the young boy to tears. It's ironic that the high-pitched laugh made famous by Tom Hulce in the 1984 film *Amadeus* would probably have made the real Mozart want to jump headfirst into the Danube River.

2

Teenage
Wasteland

The Good News about
Growing Pains

Even in the most ideal of circumstances, adolescence is a messy affair. Bodies change; voices squeak; hair grows in weird places—to say nothing of the hormonal free-for-all that shuffles moods around like a channel-surfing ninja with ADD. Teenagers have enough to deal with just being teenagers. Throw a tragedy or two into the mix, and the experience often sets them off on a pattern of unpredictability, anger, and outright rebellion.

Adolescent strife is a common story among tortured artists. The Spanish painter Salvador Dalí, for instance, lost his mother to breast cancer when he was sixteen, calling it "the greatest blow I had experienced in my life." A year later, the future dandy man of Surrealism went off to art school in Madrid, but the death of his mother, whom he "worshipped," weighed heavily on his maturing psyche. Confrontational and disruptive throughout much of his scholastic career, he was expelled from the Academia de San Fernando after he told his professors that they were unfit to judge his work.

Salvador Dalí

The following case studies feature young artists who face sudden tragedy during the most internally volatile period of their lives. When they come out on the other side, they are fully dysfunctional adults, with no shortage of trauma and turmoil to inspire their creative endeavors.

Mary Shelley
(1797–1851)

Abstract: The big chill
Birth name: Mary Wollstonecraft Godwin
Birthplace: Somers Town, London, England
Masterwork: *Frankenstein; or, The Modern Prometheus*
Demons: Death, disillusionment, and bad weather

"Invention, it must be humbly admitted, does not consist in creating out of voice, but out of chaos."
—Preface to the 1831 edition of her famous novel

The template for troubled teenage girls has undergone some cosmetic changes over the years. A half century ago, they wore black Capri pants and Bettie Page bangs; twenty years ago, they donned blue lipstick and Nine Inch Nails T-shirts; today they are typically seen prancing around in the minimal amount of clothing required to prevent people from flagging their videos on YouTube. But despite variations in the surface minutiae, the source of their angst has remained remarkably constant over the last two centuries or so. Back then, as now, teenage girls resented their stepmothers, disobeyed their fathers, had forbidden affairs with older guys, and proceeded to get knocked up, sometimes on multiple occasions, by said older guys.

In the early nineteenth century, the restless and headstrong British teenager Mary Godwin did all of these things, all before she was nineteen and all without Morrissey lyrics putting ideas into her head. Such deeds are not so remarkable, perhaps, until you consider that, before her jangle of an adolescence came to a close, she also managed to write one the most enduring novels of all time.

From her earliest years, the author of the Gothic novel *Franken-stein* was ripe for rabble-rousing, spawned from a prominent left-wing family in Regency-era London, where the hoopla of the Enlightenment was winding down and conservatism had been spreading as a backlash to progressive thinkers. Her father, William Godwin, was a radical political philosopher famous for his theory of anarchism. Her mother, Mary Wollstonecraft, founded modern feminism as we know it. No pressure there, then. Her mother also died eleven days after giving birth to her, and when her father remarried, the ensuing years of young Mary's life played out like an episode of *Degrassi Junior High* without the bad dialogue and Canadian accents.

Mary despised her new stepmother, and she rebelled with all of the you're-not-the-boss-of-me vitriol one would expect from a child of unwelcome blended surroundings. At the age of sixteen, she began an affair with Percy Bysshe Shelley, a friend of her father and hotshot poet of the Romantic age. At the time, Percy had a pregnant wife, but then he was also a kind of free-loving proto-hippie who didn't let such obligations stand in the way of his baser desires. Mary's father forbade the relationship, but his condemnation didn't stop the couple from running off to France together. In February 1815, Mary and Percy had a premature baby girl, who died less than two weeks later. The following year they had another child, a boy, and by this time Mary was already suffering from anxiety and exhaustion. Not yet nineteen, she had crammed a lifetime of turbulent experiences into her adolescence, and the combination of these experiences might seem to be enough to inspire a classic horror novel. Except that they weren't. In fact, the ultimate catalyst for Mary's literary immortality was an external catastrophe of global proportions.

In the spring of 1815, the largest volcanic eruption in recorded history blew the top off of Mount Tambora, on the Indonesian island of Sumbawa. The explosion, which killed about 10,000 people instantly, sent a massive cloud of ash and debris into the earth's atmosphere, spanning some 93 cubic miles. Months of cataclysmic weather followed the event: darkness, plummeting temperatures, endless precipitation. The freakish weather patterns devastated crops in Europe and North America, causing famine and death throughout both continents. Soon the event went from cataclysmic to apocalyptic. Food shortages sparked riots. Grain markets and bakeries became targets for arson and looting as hungry citizens, unaware of the cause of the devastation, sought out scapegoats on whom to blame the crisis.

The following year became aptly known as "the year without a summer." It was also the year, as fate would have it, that Mary and Percy went vacationing in Geneva with their friends and fellow writers, Lord Byron and John Polidori. Mary, in ill health after her second pregnancy, needed to get away, as did the debt-ridden Percy, whose extravagant lifestyle was catching up to him in the form of overzealous creditors. Unfortunately for the couple, the dismal weather put a damper on their sabbatical. "It proved a wet, ungenial summer, and incessant rain often confined us for days to the house," Mary wrote in her diary.

Holed up in their hotel, the writers entertained themselves as best as could be expected in a prewired world. In other words, they resorted to having actual conversations—discussing hot-button topics of the day, including recent scientific discoveries and the scientists who discovered them. (Inventors of the era had names that would soon be immortalized in the coming world of electricity: Alessandro Volta, James Watt, and Luigi Galvani.) Intrigued by such notions as "galvanism" or the stimulation of muscles via electric current, the friends decided to challenge themselves with a contest to see who among them could write the best ghost story. Over the next few days, Mary found herself strapped for ideas, until one night, amid the gloom of the cold summer and the horror of the most devastating famine of her century, inspiration came to her. As she put her head down to sleep, she dreamed up the concept of an obsessive scientist who creates a living being out of spare body parts: "I saw the hideous phantasm of a man stretched out, and then, on the working of some powerful engine, show signs of life, and stir with an uneasy, half-vital motion."

The novel created from that waking dream was *Frankenstein; or, The Modern Prometheus*. After some editorial direction from Percy, whom Mary married after their summer in Geneva, the book was published, anonymously, in March 1818. The story drew from elements of the Gothic and the Romantic periods, but the gloomy summer of 1816—and its influence on Mary's psyche—can be felt throughout the book.

"she dreamed up the concept of an obsessive scientist who creates a living being out of spare body parts"

In terms of longstanding cultural reach, it's hard to overstate the influence of this high-concept tale of artificial life. It stands as one of the first allegories for an electronic age, a forewarning of the coming industrial revolution and the havoc it could wreak if gone unchecked. Where have we not seen the story adapted, or paid homage to, or spoofed? Its various offshoots, motifs, and accessories belong to the masses: the bolts on Boris Karloff's neck, the short film that launched the career of filmmaker Tim Burton, the Broadway musical that made Mel Brooks think he could get away with charging $450 a ticket. For each of these dubious paragons, we can thank two major eruptions that took place nearly 200 years ago: one on a remote island in Southeast Asia and the other within the volatile psyche of a teenage girl. ∽

Irving Berlin
(1888–1989)

Abstract: Don't just stand there, busk a move
Birth name: Israel Baline
Birthplace: Unknown, somewhere in Russia
Masterwork: *White Christmas*
Demons: Indigence

"I never felt poverty, because I'd never known anything else."
—From *Billboard* magazine, 1949

Long before popular music evolved its many genres and subgenres, the industry was driven by a simple one-size-fits-all philosophy uncomplicated by impassioned debates over the origins of trip hop or the difference between deathcore and screamo. Songwriters, once upon a time, wrote songs for the masses.

Songs like "God Bless America," "White Christmas," and "There's No Business Like Show Business" are so deeply embedded within our subconscious playlists that it's hard to believe someone actually sat down to write them. In fact, the immortal tunemeister Irving Berlin wrote all three, along with about 1,500 others, not to mention the scores for eighteen Hollywood films and nineteen Broadway musicals. Few songwriters have been as instrumental in creating the mold for American music. Berlin's six-decade career began before the advent of radio and ended during the height of Beatlemania.

And although he's known for churning out the kind of era-appropriate sap that gently finesses our nostalgia lobes into submission, he did not develop his gift for pleasant melodies out of a burning need to express his inner bliss. He developed it as a survival tactic during the impoverished adolescence he spent on the streets.

Irving Berlin was born Israel Baline, the youngest of eight children in a Jewish family in a small Russian village. His exact birthplace is disputed, but then he didn't live there for very long, anyway. His only memory from Russian life was that of seeing his home burn to the ground after it was torched by the Cossacks, an unruly sect of xenophobes trained by the Russian military. In 1893, when Israel was five, the Baline family fled Russia for America, riding a wave of mass Jewish migration to New York's Lower East Side. Two months after Israel's thirteenth birthday, his father died from a vascular disease, and the Balines suddenly found themselves worse off than they had been in their impoverished homeland. His family expected him to do what all decent immigrant boys did at that time: quit school, get a job, and help support the family. He managed the quitting school part without a hitch, but he could not seem to earn the kind of money that a rapidly growing buck was expected to take in. "He contributed less than the least of his sisters," the theater critic Alexander Woollcott later noted. "He was sick with a sense of his own worthlessness."

Israel left home that year. And although he found the perilous streets of the East Village to be slightly less terrifying than a disapproving Jewish mother, the environment was still far from kind. With no education and no skills, he began singing in saloons along the Bowery, hoping the customers would fling a few pennies in his direction. The saloons were mostly populated by sailors, immigrant laborers, and prostitutes—tough crowds, to say the least. But the young Israel's pride kept him from going back to his family. In the process of sticking it out as a workaday busker, he honed a skill that would prove invaluable to him as a future purveyor of pop: the ability to please a crowd, to tap into the shared tastes of an audience, even under the toughest of circumstances. The saloon drunkards made the perfect focus group. Play something they like and you get paid; play something they hate and watch out for that flying beer mug. Israel soon discovered that the barflies responded well to popular tear-jerkers of the day, such as "The Mansion of Aching Hearts," which had a special way of subduing inebriated souls.

"he was sick with a sense of his own worthlessness"

In 1904, when Israel was sixteen, he landed a full-time job as a singing waiter at a Chinatown café, where he attracted the attention of Harry Von Tilzer, the songwriter who cowrote "Aching Hearts." Von Tilzer had recently opened his own music-publishing company, and Israel parlayed his success as a singing waiter to become one of the most widely published songwriters of the blossoming Tin Pan Alley, beginning in 1907 with the song "Marie of Sunny Italy," for which he was paid thirty-seven cents. A typo on the sheet music's cover—I. Berlin instead of I. Baline—gave Israel his stage name, and the newly christened songwriter went on to produce a slew of hits over the following decade.

When recorded music took hold in the industry, Berlin waded through the changing tides and came out on top. With recorded music came recording artists, and those artists needed songwriters to provide them with hits. Jolson, Sinatra, Holiday, Garland, Merman—Berlin's songs helped make stars out of an entire generation of songstresses and crooners.

In a 1916 interview with *The New York Times*, Berlin said he didn't believe in inspiration. Songwriting, he said, was simply the result of hard work. It was also a way for him to commemorate all that was absent from his early life. Indeed, "White Christmas," his most beloved standard, becomes especially telling from the Russian-Jewish immigrant who spent his adolescence busking for pennies in Bowery saloons. ("I didn't have a Christmas," Berlin once wrote.) The song, as recorded by Bing Crosby in 1942, remains the bestselling single of all time.

Berlin's true talent was, in the end, not musical but social, learning people's likes and dislikes and responding accordingly. It's the kind of talent best learned not at Juilliard or Eastman but in the path of a few carefully flung beer mugs. ∽

And Now This Is Happening

After Berlin's perilous adolescence on the streets, it would have been nice if his suffering days had ended. They didn't. In 1912, at the age of twenty-four, he married Dorothy Goetz. While on their honeymoon in Havana, Goetz contracted typhoid fever and died six months later. Berlin wrote the unambiguously titled "When I Lost You," his first ballad, as a means of expressing his grief. The song, at least, was a huge hit.

Arthur Miller

(1915–2005)

Abstract: Death of a status update
Birth name: Arthur Asher Miller
Birthplace: New York, New York, USA
Masterwork: *Death of a Salesman*
Demons: Financial instability

"The Depression was a crash of accepted values. You got the feeling that you were living in a very conditional world which could be swept aside in ten minutes."
—Interview with **Michigan Quarterly Review**, 2004

Rags-to-riches stories occupy a powerful—and cheerful—place in the American psyche, showing that anyone can become anything through hard work and a little luck. When we hear stories of the inverse—complacent richlings being knocked down to lower rungs on the economic ladder—we assume it is the operation of karmic justice. (Did MC Hammer really believe that the one-hit gravy train would last forever?) Rarely do such stories serve as sources of inspiration. But for Arty Miller, a lanky Jewish-American teenager growing up in New York City in the late 1920s, financial collapse was just the life lesson he needed to propel his rise as one of the giants of American drama.

Arty enjoyed an upscale life for much of his boyhood, growing up in a luxury apartment overlooking the north end of Central Park. His father, Isadore, owned a successful women's clothing store in the Garment District, where he employed some 800 people—this despite the fact that he never graduated from elementary school. Arty looked up to his father, as lads do, and images of the old man being chauffeured off to work in a limousine instilled in the young boy some very soothing, if exaggerated, notions of what it means to be a sturdy patriarch and good provider.

And yet the substratum behind the Millers' uppity lives was flimsier than anyone realized. Like many Americans of the era, Isadore invested nearly all of his wealth in the stock market, confident that an economic system based on growth would just keep growing forever. It didn't, of course, and on Black Thursday, October 24, 1929, Isadore's financial Jenga tower came crashing down along with the rest of the American economy. Overnight, the Miller family lost everything. No longer able to afford their plush Manhattan abode, they decamped to the remote stretches of Gravesend, Brooklyn, where they settled in a tiny house on a dead-end street.

Arty was fourteen at the time of the collapse, a year past his bar mitzvah and just coming to understand the nuances of economics, politics, family, and the slippery relationship between the three. That he abruptly went from upper-crust comfort to outer-borough oblivion did not sit easily. One minute he was singing songs at the family piano with his glamorous socialite of a mother; the next, he was sharing a tiny bedroom with his snoring grandfather. And yet what Arty resented most was not his change in surroundings; it was the feeling that his father, through sheer complacency and shortsightedness, had failed the family. Isadore trusted blindly in the stock market, leaving nothing under his mattress for a rainy day. His clothing store, consequently, could not survive the precipitous drop in consumer spending, and he was eventually forced to shut down the entire operation.

Arty watched in quiet angst as his mother pawned off her expensive furs and jewelry. As the once-stylish woman grew more and more miserable by her loss of social standing, Arty became more and more resentful toward the father he believed was responsible for the mess.

Of course, Arty's story would hardly be distinguishable from that of countless other Depression-era Americans had he not grown up to become Arthur Miller the Playwright. Many of his plays—*All My Sons*, *The Crucible*, *A View from the Bridge*—remain theater standards to this day. But it's in *Death of a Salesman*, the story of a door-to-door hawker who is unexpectedly demoted at the twilight of his career, that we

"overnight, the Miller family lost everything"

can see Miller playing out the financial trauma and paternal letdown of his teenage years. The play's lead character, the blistered and broken Willy Loman, is as much a disappointment to his wife and sons as Isadore was to the Millers. Willy, like Isadore, was also blinded by self-delusion. As a younger man, he believed in the potential of his own greatness, but he lacked the wile to outsmart the real world, which tends to smack you around a few times before it grants you a pass to greater fortunes. And just as Isadore entrusted his future to the tottering bubble of Wall Street, so Willy entrusted his to the salesman vocation that ultimately crushed his will to live. Willy Loman represented a new kind of antihero, and his shortcomings shined a light on all the Willy Lomans of midcentury America— the workaday stiffs who sold their souls for a piece of the American dream only to find themselves wishing they had kept the receipt.

Death of a Salesman was a critical and commercial hit when it opened in 1949. Twenty years after the crash on Wall Street, Arthur had channeled his experiences onto the stage to great critical acclaim. The play won a Tony Award and a New York Drama Critics' Circle

Award, for best play, as well as the Pulitzer Prize for Drama. Willy Loman remains an archetype of the failed American patriarch, and *Death of a Salesman*, a parable for the failed American dream—a bitter lead balloon with which Arthur Miller was all too familiar. "The presumption of a permanent prosperity exploded in a matter of weeks," he once said of the crash that upended his life. "It was an earthquake that changed what America thought of itself." ∽

Marlon Brando

(1924–2004)

Abstract: The madness and the Method
Birth name: Marlon Brando Jr.
Birthplace: Omaha, Nebraska, USA
Peak Performance: As Stanley Kowalski in *A Streetcar Named Desire,* Ethel Barrymore Theatre, opening night, December 3, 1947
Demons: Anger

"Acting is the expression of a neurotic impulse. It's a bum's life."
—**To his biographer, Gary Carey**

If there is a single prototype for the rogue celebrity, it would have to be Marlon Brando, whose open contempt for Hollywood and utter lack of respect for his own profession made him one of the most notorious stars of his generation. The churlish actor was wholly incapable of engaging in the kind of pleasantries on which the movie industry is built. Yet, despite the fact that he probably never did a lunch in his life, he commanded almost universal respect among his peers due to his unmatched mastery of the craft of acting—which is not to say that he believed there was much to master. "I laugh at people who call moviemaking an 'art' and actors 'artists,'" he once scoffed.

Evidence of Marlon's defiant core was seen as far back as his early days as a rambunctious toddler, when he had to be taken to kindergarten on a leash. The strong and spirited little boy had no positive influences to help channel his energy into a constructive outlet. His strict and abusive father was often absent. His hard-drinking mother worked late nights at a community theater, leaving Marlon in the care of his very affectionate nurse, Ermeline—a stunning Dane who at the time was his whole world. Not only did the two of them sleep together in the nude, but Ermeline even occasionally let the five-year-old Marlon fondle her breasts. It was all well and good until Ermeline left to get married. The young Marlon felt betrayed and abandoned, and soon his energetic antics progressed to blatant rancor.

By the time Marlon reached adolescence, his energy had festered into a simmering pot of rage, aimed largely at his father, who claimed to live by "The Good Book" but then ran around with other women while Marlon's mother drank herself into a stupor. Marlon was infuriated by his father's blatant hypocrisy, and one night in 1936, his fury came to a boil when Marlon's mother caught her husband with lipstick on his underpants and became frantic. Rather than apologize for his transgression, Marlon's father took his wife into the bedroom and started beating her. Marlon, then twelve, rushed in and threatened to kill his father if he ever laid a finger on her again. It would not be the last altercation between the two. With Marlon living under the constant threat of a brawl with his old man, it's little wonder how he became imbued with his famously short fuse. His intractable rage marked his teen years with a steady stream of blow-ups and expulsions. In the early 1940s, Marlon's disruptive behavior got him kicked out of two high schools. It was then that he decided to leave the family farm in Libertyville, Illinois, and head to New York City to study theater.

"Theater?" Marlon's father snapped. "That's for faggots. It's not man's work."

Of course, no yokel-in-the-city story would be complete without a mentor, and Marlon found his in the renowned acting teacher Stella Adler, who quickly picked up on his uncanny ability to mimic the mannerisms and facial expressions of anybody he wanted. "He takes in everything," she said of Marlon's chameleon-like gifts, "including the size of your teeth."

But training Marlon for the stage would be no small task. There was, after all, still the problem of his uncooperative nature. Marlon butted heads with directors, fellow actors, and pretty much everyone else. No ordinary teacher could have whipped him into shape, but then Adler was no ordinary teacher. Years earlier, she had studied with Konstantin Stanislavski, the Russian stage director credited with turning acting into a bona fide craft. Stanislavski stressed a naturalistic technique whereby actors draw from their real-life experiences to create realistic performances. Adler was the only American actor ever to study personally with Stanislavski. She, along with Harold Clurman and Lee Strasberg, were instrumental in popularizing his technique in New York City, where it eventually became known as Method acting.

> "not only did the two of them sleep together in the nude, but Ermeline even occasionally let the five-year-old Marlon fondle her breasts"

The Method, as it turned out, was ideal for Marlon. Whereas his entire life had been about bottling up his anger only to have it explode at the worst possible times, Adler taught him to channel his rage, to save it for when it counted—namely, his performances. Her tough-love training equipped him with the tools to tackle the role of the brutish and ballistic Stanley Kowalski in *A Streetcar Named Desire,* a new Broadway play by Tennessee Williams. Stanley was id on parade, loutish and animalistic yet powerful and magnetic. *Streetcar* producers were not convinced that the role should go to the relatively unknown Brando, but when Marlon auditioned for Williams personally, the playwright nearly popped his cataract in response to the actor's explosive characterization.

And Williams would not be alone in his reaction. *Streetcar* opened on Broadway in 1947, and the twenty-four-year-old Brando blew audiences away. "Our expectations of what an actor should offer us in the way of psychological truth and behavioral honesty were forever changed," beamed *Time* magazine.

With Broadway success, Hollywood offers predictably followed, but Marlon treated them with flagrant disregard. (For one Warner Brothers screen test, he demonstrated how to eat a raw egg on camera.) He saw himself as a theater actor, trained within New York intellectual circles that still looked down on movies as a lower art form. And he might have stayed in those circles forever had doing so not proven to be too painful. As *Streetcar* performances rolled on, Marlon became more and more exhausted by the intensely demonstrative process. Playing Stanley required a journey into the depths of his own rage, but at eight performances a week, the trips were nearly debilitating. "Try to imagine," he wrote in his autobiography, "what it was like walking on a stage at 8:30 every night having to yell, scream, cry, break dishes, kick the furniture, punch the walls and *experience* the same intense, wrenching emotions."

Stanley Kowalski would not only be Marlon's greatest stage role; it would be his last. In 1954, he starred in a film version of *Streetcar,* and when it became a hit, Marlon vowed to never do Broadway again. "I've never had any respect for Hollywood," he said, admitting himself a sellout. "But when you act in a movie, you act for three months and then you can do what you want for the rest of the year."

It was Marlon's ability to channel his pain into his performances that made him a great actor. But it was his inability to relive that pain night after night that made him a movie star. His screen career brought Method acting to a whole new level of exposure, paving the way for legendary Methodological shenanigans from Robert De Niro's raging-bull bulge to Joaquin Phoenix's incoherent ramblings on *Letterman*. Marlon may not have considered acting an art form, but he legitimized it as one in the eyes of the world.

Nevertheless, he never softened his stance on acting, especially his own. Even his now-mythologized performance as Vito Corleone, in the 1972 film *The Godfather*, gave him the creeps: "When I saw it the first time, it made me sick." And although he continued to act until his death at the age of eighty, there was rarely a sense that his latter roles meant anything more to him than a paycheck. Some critics cite his overpaid role as Jor-El, in the 1978 film version of *Superman*, as the epitome of Brando's depleted soul. But there is a kind of poetic parallel buried within the story of that film's superhuman protagonist: Clark Kent, from humble beginnings, ditches the family farm, heads to the big city, and emerges a superhero. It has a familiar ring. ~

John Hughes
(1950–2009)

Abstract: An ounce of detention
Birth name: John Wilden Hughes Jr.
Birthplace: Lansing, Michigan, USA
Masterwork: *The Breakfast Club*
Demons: Privilege and disadvantage

"I was grimly serious in my teen and college years."
—Interview with *The New York Times*, 1991

In the summer of 1962, the Hughes family of Grosse Point, Michigan, relocated to Northbrook, Illinois, an uppity Chicago suburb. The Hugheses were not an uppity family. If a middle-class spectrum can be said to exist, then they surely fell on the lower end. Their twelve-year-old son, John, was understandably anxious about starting at a new school populated by the privileged locals, and his unease proved completely warranted. That fall, he found himself in a confusing maze of angst, melodrama, heartbreak, and indivisible social cliques—all of which is a way of saying that John Hughes found himself in a John Hughes movie.

To anyone born after the American baby boom, that description bears no explanation. The twelve-year-old new kid who navigated high school life as an outsider in an upscale North Shore neighborhood would grow up to have an astounding effect on the juvenility of 1980s cinema.

Hughes's obsession with the histrionics of Reagan-era high schoolers breathed new life into the teen-movie genre, which began in earnest with *Rebel Without a Cause* but fizzled into smutty self-parody somewhere around *Porky's II*.

At first glance, John Hughes's own high school identity was ostensibly more Ferris Bueller than Samantha Baker. He was basically a charming, good-looking lad, adored by sportos, wasteoids, and motorheads alike. His encyclopedic knowledge of pop culture marked him as an odd duck, but not in an overly geeky way. In a pre-Internet world, he was the human search engine you could go to for details about last week's episode of *Flipper*. But while John got along fine with all the cliques, he never really belonged to one. His move to the outskirts of McMansion-land made him acutely aware of his place on the lower end of the middle-class umbrella—a distinction that fostered in him a deep resentment of the snobbery and elitism that existed all around him.

As much difficulty as John had trying to connect at school, he had an even more difficult time at home. His parents thought his creative endeavors were a waste of time. When John told them he wanted to study art, they dismissed the idea, thinking instead that he should pursue a safer career in business. John majored in art at the University of Arizona, but he dropped out after only one year. Upon his return to Northbrook, he rounded up all his paintings and threw them on the sidewalk for trash pickup.

It was during this transitional year when John realized the true unfairness of the proverbial tracks that divided his suburban town and how people born on the right side of those tracks never seemed to appreciate, or deserve, the cushy futures that were mapped out for them. Two decades later, John would proclaim in an interview, "I just don't care for birthright," but it was the year he turned twenty, while he was working in a warehouse, that those words came into sharp focus. John Hughes, the perpetual outsider, had no birthright, and no one was going to hand him anything.

That being the case, John climbed the creative ladder from a ground-level rung, starting out as a freelance joke writer and clawing his way up to a staff position at *National Lampoon* magazine. One of his humor stories, "Vacation '58," proved so popular that he was given the chance to adapt it into a screenplay, and suddenly John had gone from freelance joke writer to Hollywood screenwriter. But that experience only caused him further resentment, as he watched his scripts mutate through the infamous channels of development hell.

The only solution, of course, would be to convince someone to let him direct his own project, but such an opportunity seemed unlikely in that he barely knew how to work a camera. That was when John realized the truth: He would have to conceive of a movie so ridiculously simple that even *he* could make it.

"he found himself in a confusing maze of angst, melodrama, heartbreak, and indivisible social cliques"

John wrote incessantly for the next three days, and when he came up for air, he had completed the first draft of a script called *Detention*, about five suburban high school students—all from different social cliques—who spend a Saturday detention together. It was set almost entirely in one room. It required only a small cast of young, inexperienced actors, who would be more likely to take direction without talking back. For an amateur auteur, it was the perfect project. However, when John pitched it, the studios were less than enthused. A teen movie with no sex? No parties? No locker-room nudity? "Kids won't sit through it!" bellowed one producer.

John went back to the drawing board and devised a more commercial concept. This one had all the teen-movie clichés that 1980s studio execs had brainlessly come to expect: unrequited love, drunken driving, a parentless party at a house wrapped in toilet paper, and, of course, the requisite school dance. The movie was called *Sixteen Candles,* and while it wore the outward face of typical teenage raunchfest, its honest treatment of teen issues instantly stood out. Critics took notice of the fact that John actually seemed to care about the problems modern teenagers faced. According to Roger Ebert, *Sixteen Candles* didn't "hate its characters or condescend to them, the way a lot of teenage movies do."

What critics did not realize was that John, barely thirty-four, was forming an unusual bond with his young actors: Molly Ringwald, Anthony Michael Hall, and the other future Brat Packers were a surrogate family that understood him in a way that the parents who dismissed his creative endeavors never could. Nowhere is this divide more apparent than in John's original detention script, produced a year later as *The Breakfast Club.* The film's five lead characters, for all their differences, share one common trait: They all come from miserable home lives. Thus the privileged rich girl is revealed to be an unloved pawn in her parents' divorce. The brainy nerd is a tortured overachiever who would sooner shoot himself than show mom and dad a tarnished report card. The wise-ass hoodlum is a fearful child of abuse with a cigar-size burn to prove it. The competitive jock is a people pleaser who taped Larry Lester's buns together to impress his alpha-male father. And then there's Allison, the oddball loner, who admits to being so neglected at home that she is starved for attention.

It's that last character with whom John Hughes admitted that he most identified. From his own teen years in the divided North Shore suburb that would inspire his fictional Shermer, Illinois, John had always believed himself to be an outsider. And when he finally found success as a filmmaker, that identity only intensified. He lived in Hollywood for only a few years before retreating to a farm outside Chicago. Indeed, when he died suddenly of a heart attack on a Manhattan street, in 2009, the news of his death felt like the first time we'd heard his name in more than fifteen years. Looking back, however, his teen movies have aged remarkably well, standing not only as a time capsule for the era of leggings and sweater vests but also as a timeless dictum of the American teenage experience. ～

3

Perpetual Virginity

Unrequited Love and the Tortured Artist (or, Your Muse Is Just Not That Into You)

"There is always some madness in love," wrote Friedrich Nietzsche, "but there is also always some reason in madness." Modern research suggests that love is, literally, a form of madness. One study by the University of California, San Diego, revealed that the brain patterns of the love struck are almost identical to those who suffer from obsessive-compulsive disorder. Pine over your beloved or comb the fringes out of your rug; your brain doesn't know the difference.

Despite the irrational effects of Cupid's arrow, we really have no cogent means to defend ourselves against it. There is no bargaining with love. The brain's feeble voice of reason is useless against the heart's all-encompassing pangs of desire. This is not always a bad thing. If the person on the receiving end returns our love, we can expect to enjoy one of those happy endings that feel so disgustingly schmaltzy in Kate Hudson movies. However, when our love is not returned, our egos will just as forcefully cry out for validation. For tortured artists, unrequited love can launch entire careers, as was the case with the budding novelist Ayn Rand, who, years before she wrote *The Fountainhead*, had a love affair with a free-spirited young man who did not return her feelings. Rand was too hurt by the experience to publicly reveal the fellow's identity, but she used him as the inspiration for Leo Kovalensky, the handsome love interest of her first published novel, *We the Living*.

Eric Clapton

Three decades later, in 1970, Eric Clapton skyrocketed to fame with the now-classic song "Layla." The guitar virtuoso had fallen hopelessly in love with the mod fashion model Pattie Boyd, but the blueberry-eyed beauty was already married to his good friend George Harrison. Clapton realized that the only way to compete with a Beatle was to write a hit song, and apparently it worked: Boyd left Harrison in 1974 and married Clapton in 1979.

When unrequited love strikes the lives of artists, it often does so early, before they have achieved success. It happens before the fame, the admiration, the yes men. In other words, it happens when they are the most vulnerable to rejection. But ultimately the experience can inspire an artist's most defining works. The following stories reveal how masterpieces can be shaped by a fleeting romance, a torrid affair, or even a simple crush.

Dante Alighieri
(1265–1321)

Abstract: Stalk like a man
Birth name: Durante degli Alighieri
Birthplace: Florence, Italy
Masterwork: *The Divine Comedy*
Demons: Love and war

"Oh, misery . . . I will often be troubled from now on."
—From *La Vita Nuova*, 1295

It should come as no surprise that the man who conceptualized our modern view of eternal damnation had a few personal demons, but Dante Alighieri was far more tortured than your garden-variety medieval wordsmith. As an influential versifier, Italy's *Sommo Poeta* ("the Supreme Poet") is often compared with Homer or Shakespeare, but as a young poet on the streets of Florence, he was simply a hopeless romantic who drew much of his inspiration from the accidental temptress Beatrice Portinari, a girl he barely knew.

Dante first laid eyes on this "glorious lady" at a May Day bash when he was nine and Beatrice was eight, and he spotted her all dolled up in a crimson dress. "From then on," he fawned, "I say that Amor governed my soul." If the thought of the Roman god of love governing the soul of an eight-year-old boy seems excessive, it helps to place the quote in context, meaning the Middle Ages, when courtly love was more fashionable than creepy. Nine years later, Dante crossed paths with Beatrice again, this time on the street, where she greeted him as she passed by. That brief encounter threw him into a veritable whirlwind of emotional expression.

"I left the crowd as if intoxicated," he later wrote. "I returned to the solitude of my own room, and fell to thinking of this most gracious one." Dante claimed to have met Beatrice only on these two occasions, and yet the brevity of their encounters did not stop him from making her his lifelong muse. Given this proclivity for unsolicited devotion, it's tempting to liken Dante to that guy who kept getting arrested for stalking Uma Thurman, but whether his affections for Beatrice arose from true love or an untreated chemical imbalance makes little difference seven centuries onward. To Dante,

"that brief encounter threw him into a veritable whirlwind of emotional expression"

Beatrice was an ideal, a quasi-religious experience through which he came to wrap his head around such abstract concepts as truth, purity, and undying love.

The first catalyst for Dante's inner torment was Beatrice's sudden death at the age of twenty-four, the cause of which remains a mystery. That incident sent the poet into a creative frenzy, and he spent the next three years composing love poetry in Beatrice's honor (an obsession that no doubt irritated his wife, Gemma). The collection of verse eventually became the book *La Vita Nuova*, which marked a momentous step forward in the development of Dante's poetry. In it, Dante retells his personal story of unrequited love and the transformative journey on which it had taken him. His early encounters with

Beatrice spark lustful yearnings, causing Dante despair and shame. Following her death, however, he undergoes a spiritual renewal of sorts, with his love for the girl taking its most idealized form.

Unfortunately, just as Dante seemed to be working through his issues, he suffered a second mental wound, this one inflicted not by love but politics. As a man of esteemed social status, he was heavily involved in Florentine affairs. However, Italian city-states tended to be quite volatile, and Dante, being of a liberal slant, found himself on the wrong side of a fierce political divide. When his political party, the White Guelphs, lost control to the more radical Black Guelphs, the poet was sentenced to exile and condemned to be burned alive if he were ever to show his face in Florence again. The sentence was devastating to the patriotic Dante, who spent the next few years aligning with other outcasts in hopes of regaining power. When those alliances proved fruitless, Dante grew increasingly disillusioned by the ineptitude of his fellow exiles. It's no coincidence that around this same time he began work on *Inferno*, the first—and darkest—canticle of *The Divine Comedy*, a three-part masterpiece that would propel him into the literary stratosphere and help give birth to the modern Italian language. Here Dante demonstrated the sort of self-obsession common among tortured artists when, in a cutting-edge play on structure, he made *himself* the hero of his own epic. Such an Everyman formula was unheard of at a time when protagonists were generally written as Schwarzenegger-esque warriors. *Inferno* recounts the hero's journey through nine circles of Hell, with each circle holding more astringent punishments for more severe sinners. Fittingly, Dante reserved the final and most caustic circle of Hell for traitors, as the author likely enjoyed placing those responsible for his exile in the domain closest to Lucifer himself.

Dante revived Beatrice one last time in *Purgatorio* and *Paradiso*. His lifelong object of desire appears in these canticles as his personal tour guide through heaven, apparently the only being pure enough to get past the bouncer. It's here that all traces of the historical Beatrice are lost, and she transforms into a pure work of fiction—an allegory of virtue and goodness dreamed up by the author's fertile imagination. In contrast to Dante the unrequited romantic, there was, one assumes, an antipodal version of the man, a dedicated husband and father of four who was secretly consumed by the things he could not have. Of course, any comment on his wife, Gemma, would be pure speculation. Public records from the era are scarce, and Dante, for all his writings, never mentioned her once. ∿

Nine Circles of Dante's *Personal* Hell

One: His mother dies when he's only seven.

Two: He falls in love with Beatrice at the age of nine. Unfortunately, he's too young to do anything about it.

Three: At twelve, he's arranged to be married to Gemma Donati, despite the fact that he's still hung up on Beatrice.

Four: At twenty-four, he fights in the Battle of Campaldino and learns that, um, war is hell.

Five: He goes on a writing binge upon Beatrice's death and writes *La Vita Nuova*.

Six: His political party falls out of favor; he gets booted out of Florence.

Seven: He takes part in failed attempts to regain power.

Eight: He becomes a disillusioned loner after prolonged exile.

Nine: He gets in touch with his bitterness and begins work on what will become *The Divine Comedy*.

Jane Austen
(1775–1817)

Abstract: Tales from the snark side
Birth name: Jane Austen
Birthplace: Hampshire, England
Masterwork: *Pride and Prejudice*
Demons: The marriage machine

"I do not want people to be agreeable, as it saves me the trouble of liking them."
—In a letter to her sister, December 24, 1798

In an effort to uncover details of Jane Austen's personal life, curious biographers are often left scratching their Regency bonnets. It seems that despite the endless Austen Societies, BBC Miniseries, and cheeky zombie parodies, we really don't know very much about the real facts surrounding the life of this endlessly popular chick-lit pioneer. We know from her fiction, of course, that she possessed a sublime wit and was critical of the conventions of her era, particularly the fact that marrying for money was pretty much the only option available to young women. However, getting to know Jane herself, and what punishing imperfections may have chipped away at her psyche, is a puzzling affair.

Approaching this quandary, one might logically begin with Jane's looks, which would have been a defining characteristic in a society ruled by a woman-as-commodity mindset. Unfortunately, the author's appearance is shrouded in as much uncertainty as her private life. The only authenticated image of her is a watercolor/pencil sketch drawn by her older sister, Cassandra, when Jane was in her thirties. The sketch is decidedly prosaic, casting Jane as a thin-lipped spinster with apparent facial edema. It's also a stark contrast to the bright-eyed Anne Hathaway, who portrayed Jane in Julian Jarrold's 2007 film, *Becoming Jane,* but then Hollywood is famous for such revisionist makeovers. (Does anyone really believe Jesse James looked like Brad Pitt?) Still, while Jarrold's film

> "the status-driven Irishman could not have been very serious about a penniless country girl"

no doubt took liberties with Jane's appearance, its central focus—namely her ill-fated romance with the Irishman Tom Lefroy—gets to the root of the author's tortured soul.

Jane Austen and Tom Lefroy were both just twenty years old when they met over the Christmas season of 1795, he a hotshot law grad on his way up the ladder, and she a small-town girl of modest means.

Literary types tend to squabble over the seriousness of the couple's involvement. Jarrold's film, like the book that inspired it, envisions Jane and Lefroy in a passionate, reciprocal affair, one savagely cut short by differences in social status. Other historians believe Jane's strong feelings for Lefroy were unreturned, insisting that the status-driven Irishman could not have been very serious about a penniless country girl. This latter theory is bolstered by the fact that Lefroy married a well-heeled heiress three years after he and Jane said their goodbyes.

Ultimately, it isn't relevant whether Lefroy was truly smitten or just out slumming it for the holidays. The relationship, for what it was, had a profound impact on Jane, and its emotionally wrenching repercussions worked their way into her literary legacy. Consider poor Marianne Dashwood, the romantically challenged heroine of *Sense and Sensibility*, who is crushed when the dashing John Willoughby passes her over for a richer prospect. Evidence of Lefroy's influence can also be found by looking at Jane's creative output: The author was extremely productive in the period following her brief romance, completing three novels in just four years. Two of these, *Sense and Sensibility* and *Pride and Prejudice*, are by far her most beloved. (The third, *Northanger Abbey*, is known colloquially as "the one nobody reads," but let's not split hairs.)

Jane Austen's popularity has grown considerably since her death. In book clubs around the world, dutiful Janites converge with regularity to exchange their admiration for the author's work. The mere fact that

"A Lady" in Waiting

Jane's long journey to see her work in print:

1795. Inspiration: Jane pens three novels in four years. For entertainment, she reads the books aloud to her family, who fortunately have no mobile devices to distract them.

1797. Rejection: Jane's father pitches *Pride and Prejudice* (original title *First Impressions*) to the publisher Thomas Cadell, who quickly rejects the query. Two centuries later, Cadell is still believed to be kicking himself.

1801. Depression: When her father retires, Jane is forced to move to the hopping resort town of Bath. The move is traumatic for the country girl; over the next decade, she barely writes a word.

1811. Publication: Jane's brother finally finds a publisher for *Sense and Sensibility*, which had been written thirteen years prior. Because female writers (or, rather, female professionals of any kind) were looked down on in those days, Jane uses the pseudonym "A Lady."

1813. Vindication: *Sensibility* sells some 750 copies. (The average middle schooler gets more follows than that on Twitter nowadays, but it was a lot for back then.) Jane, unmarried and still dependent on her brothers for support, finally wins a taste of financial freedom.

she has spawned a namesake sect of doting fans puts Jane in the company of such cultural institutions as *Star Trek* and the Grateful Dead. The irreverent Lizzy Bennet would probably scoff at such comparisons, but they're impressive to us mere mortals nonetheless. ∾

W. B. Yeats
(1865–1939)

Abstract: The mourning after
Birth name: William Butler Yeats
Birthplace: Dublin, Ireland
Masterwork: *The Wild Swans at Coole*
Demons: An incendiary giantess

"The tragedy of sexual intercourse is the perpetual virginity of the soul."
—Interview with the literary critic John Sparrow, 1931

In December 1908, the Irish poet W. B. Yeats woke up in a spacious loft on Rue de Passy, in Paris, snuggling comfortably next to Maud Gonne, the feminist and Irish nationalist whom he had long pursued. A liaison had transpired the night before, the particulars of which Yeats and Gonne took to their graves, but it was no ordinary affair by any definition. Rather, it was the culmination of a cat-and-mouse game that had persisted for nearly two decades. Yeats had almost given up. He had proposed to Maud, fruitlessly, more times than he cared to count, only to submit to her insistence that their very close friendship remain unencumbered by physical affection. In other words, Maud had adopted the same stance as the female pals of many a brace-toothed geek: Why spoil a perfectly good friendship with sex? Yeats knew then, as geeks know today, that such a question is ridiculously rhetorical.

But persistence pays, or so the story goes, and conventional wisdom has it that Maud finally gave in to his physical advances that night. "The long years of fidelity were finally rewarded," as one of Yeats's former lovers later said. Rare in the annals of poet/muse relations is a story of such blissful triumph. The whole thing would seem even sweeter had it not left Yeats himself feeling beaten, betrayed, and pierced with regret for the rest of his life.

"Yeats knew then, as geeks know today, that such a question is ridiculously rhetorical"

W. B. Yeats—or Willie, as Maud referred to him—first met Maud Gonne in 1889. Barely twenty-four, the young poet was an idealistic anti-industrialist who preferred Celtic myths and the occult to steam engines and electricity. Maud was a fan of his ethereal poetry, but she did not share his ethereal nature. She was opinionated, politically minded, fiercely intelligent, and an imposing presence in every quantifiable sense—a 6'-tall Amazon who fought tirelessly for Ireland's independence from Great Britain. Her boxy jaw, thin lips, and knotty hair were not particularly idealized by Victorian tastemakers (in pictures she looks like a cross between Bea Arthur and the bass player from Twisted Sister), but Willie saw something irresistible in her nonetheless. Over the course of his career, he produced volumes of verse and prose in her honor. However, he broke from the Dantesque tradition of muse worship that would have relegated him to humble stalkerdom. Willie was not content to worship Maud from afar, and he chased her with all the hormone-fueled purpose of an Irish wolfhound.

Throughout their decades-long friendship, he made a waggish habit of proposing to her, and she made equal sport of turning him down, claiming a fixed opposition to the institution of marriage. And although Willie and Maud shared the dream of an independent Ireland, they had different ideas about how such a dream could be brought about. Willie expressed himself with words; Maud was a woman of action who organized protests, founded women's groups, and used such expressions as "the first principle of war is to kill the enemy." Still, there was always an undeniable attraction between her and Willie, as evidenced by that night in Paris. Much to Yeats's dismay, however, it changed nothing. He may have won her body for a night, but he had not captured her heart.

The following day, Maud wrote Willie a letter, insisting that he move on for good. "Loving you as I do," she wrote, "I have prayed and I am praying still that the bodily desire for me may be taken from you." If that sounds like a mixed message, welcome to Willie's hell. While he had grown accustomed to her refusals, there was something even more humiliating about being shot down on the day after their shared night.

Eight years would pass before Willie would propose to Maud again (we knew it was coming), only to have her refuse him one final time. It was 1916. Ireland was roiled in a fight for its very soul, and Maud was pushing fifty, the years of activism showing on her creased face. Yeats, no spring chicken himself, wanted to produce an heir, and with Maud unwilling to oblige, he went for the next best thing. He proposed to Maud's daughter, Iseult (the product of an on-again-off-again affair between Maud and a French journalist), who was now twenty-one years old. Iseult admitted to a girlish crush on the famous writer, but in the end she carried on her mother's tradition by turning him down flat.

For Yeats, the double rejection, coupled with the conflict in his native country, caused a midlife crisis that would change the direction of his poetry and his legacy. The following year, he published the collection *The Wild Swans at Coole*, marking a transition into the late-career writing for which he is largely remembered. Gone was the naive escapist preoccupied with Celtic myths. Yeats, embattled from the insatiability of his long-unfulfilled desires, had matured. The new poems reflected on mortality, on death, on the struggle to find beauty in a cold world as our bodies age and decay before our eyes. (The collection's title refers to a wedge of swans that lived on a property Yeats had been visiting for nineteen years. He marvels at how, in all that time, the swans' "hearts have not grown old.") Yeats is unusual among modern poets in that he was really quite a late bloomer, producing most of his well-known works between the ages of fifty and seventy-five. His was not the voice of brash, youthful ruminations but rather of a cultivated sage whose slow path to wisdom was obtained through decades of deep self-analysis. In that regard, he owes a debt to a rejection that spanned twenty years and two generations of women.

And what of that one night in Paris? It stands, in hindsight, not as a vindication but a cautionary tale. Yeats broke Golden Rule One for unrequited love: Keep it unrequited. Some couples are simply better off apart. Whether or not Yeats and Gonne fully consummated their relationship that night, we can never really be sure, but Yeats, in later years, nearly affirmed as much with his increasing cynicism toward lust. Sexual intercourse, he said, always ends in failure, if only because the act inherently takes place on one side of the gulf that "separates the one and the many, or if you like, God and man."

Yeats did eventually have two children, although suffice it to say, they were not Maud's. And yet, in a way, his and Maud's unusual relationship did spawn an heir: Ireland itself. Maud's activism helped bring about an independent nation while Yeats, under her spell, emerged as one of its foremost literary figures. He was a new voice for a new republic, fueling an innate gift for lyricism with a lifetime of longing and sadness. It doesn't get more Irish than that. ∽

Charles M. Schulz
(1922–2000)

Abstract: Win, lose, and draw
Birth name: Charles Monroe Schulz
Birthplace: Minneapolis, Minnesota, USA
Masterwork: *Peanuts*
Demons: Rejection

"You never do get over your first love. The whole of you is rejected when a woman says, 'You're not worth it.'"
—**Interview with the *Star Tribune*, 1997**

In 1945, Charles M. Schulz, twenty-three and fresh out of the army, took a job as a teacher at Art Instruction, a learn-by-mail art school in Minneapolis. It wasn't the most prestigious job in the art world. The school was, and still is, known mostly for its long-running "Draw Me!" ad campaign, which invited would-be artists to sketch the likenesses of various cartoon characters in profile—Tippy the Turtle, Cubby the Bear, that weird pirate, and so forth. In art-education circles, Art Instruction is regarded as something akin to those x-ray glasses you used to get from the back of comic books, promising more than it delivers. But for Charles, then an aspiring cartoonist, it was an exciting stepping stone, a chance for a real career in art. Four years later, he was still teaching there, still toiling away in obscurity, when a diversion entered his workplace. Her name was Donna Mae Johnson, the new girl in accounting.

Charles was instantly drawn to Donna, and how could he not be? She was an ideal midcentury catch, a confection of Rockwellian peach skin, cherubic cheeks, and bright red hair. She was also, as luck would have it, looking to settle down. At twenty-one, she was already seven months older than the median age of marriage for women in Harry Truman's America.

Charles was one of two eligible bachelors whom she considered worthy prospects. Unfortunately for Charles, the other bachelor was Donna's high school sweetheart, Alan Wold, a hardworking, over-protective, at times jealous sort, who was studying to become a fire-fighter. Donna dated both men, simultaneously, for several months, but she became more partial to Wold as time went on. Who could blame her? Firefighters are the closest thing we have to real-life superheroes, and aspiring cartoonists, more often than not, end up sketching tourists in Atlantic City. But it wasn't Charles's limited earning potential that cooled Donna off; it was his shyness. He was a terminal introvert, sweet and well intentioned but too reserved for his own good, and he was worlds away from the assertive alpha male with whom Donna had always pictured herself.

Charles had been a passive observer in the rituals of courtship for most of his life. He did not so much pursue members of the opposite sex as observe them, quietly, from a safe distance, often developing a focused admiration for women he considered unapproachable.

Donna was Charles's first love—the first reciprocal relationship in the life of a young man who lost his mother at twenty and was still living at home at twenty-seven.

And on the night of June 14, 1950, he excitedly told her that he had just signed a deal to develop a cartoon strip for United Feature Syndicate. Armed with the newly minted promise of a bright future in cartooning, Charles at once overcame the vexing fear of rejection that had prevented him from approaching women his entire life. He asked for Donna's hand in marriage, but his proposal did not evoke the response he had hoped. In fact, she refused Charles outright, stating to the effect that she did not want to marry him or anyone else. "I just want everyone to leave me alone," she blurted. Four months later, she married Alan Wold.

Charles Schulz's future in cartooning was, of course, more than bright. His *Peanuts* comic strip, which he drew from 1950 until shortly before his death in 2000, grew to become the most successful comic strip of all time. At its peak, it appeared in about 2,600 newspapers worldwide, reaching an audience of more than 355 million people. It's hard to imagine any comic

> "she was an ideal midcentury catch, a confection of Rockwellian peach skin, cherubic cheeks, and bright red hair"

strip achieving such a reach today, even if we were to ignore the obvious observation that the world probably doesn't have 2,600 newspapers left in it. And yet *Peanuts* spread far beyond its funny-page roots. It spawned movies, TV specials, stage plays, books, and endless merchandising. There is no medium, no Macy's parade, no MetLife blimp that the strip did not infiltrate.

At the core of its success have always been Charles Schulz's multifaceted neuroses, expressed to exhaustion in the strip's antithetical hero, Charlie Brown, the mustard-shirted born loser with a masochistic need for endless self-reflection. Charlie Brown was a sloping Everykid, who sought acceptance from his peers, got depressed around the holidays, and blew off homework to play baseball only to then beat himself up for procrastinating. *Peanuts* presented childhood as it really is: full of misery and loneliness.

However, the one theme in the strip that stood out above the rest was rejection. The characters could feel love, but they were never loved back, and Schulz took great pains to make sure it always stayed that way. Thus Sally's girlhood crush on Linus was never returned, Lucy's curt advances toward Schroeder were always futile, and Peppermint Patty and Marcie never realized how perfect a lesbian couple they really made. Then there was Charlie Brown himself, who spent countless school lunches alone on a bench, pining hopelessly for the Little Red-Haired Girl. This character, only seen through Charlie Brown's point of view, is the manifestation of the redheaded secretary who passed Charles over for another guy. In a 1997 interview he even named her by name, explaining how he never really got over the sting. "I can think of no more emotionally damaging loss than to be turned down by someone you love," Schulz said. "A person who not only turns you down, but almost immediately will marry the victor. What a bitter blow that is."

Donna herself has also been interviewed on the topic, saying that she has no regrets over her decision. And although she may claim not to wonder about what might have been, let's face it, she does. *Peanuts* is a masterpiece of minimalism, a pen-and-ink Greek tragedy through which the simplest drawings expose the harrowing experience that is childhood. It's impossible not to think about how different the strip would have been had she said yes that night in 1950. Imagine Charlie Brown getting some tongue. It doesn't quite work. ∽

Till Death Do Us Part

Charles Schulz was never coy about the fact that he and Charlie Brown were alter egos. They shared the same first name, their dads were both barbers, and they were both endlessly melancholy. But the eeriest commonality between the two might have been their last. When Schulz announced his retirement in December 1999, he requested that United Feature Syndicate discontinue *Peanuts* after his death. He drew enough Sunday strips to last only through mid-February, and on Saturday, February 12, 2000, he passed away. The final *Peanuts* strip was printed, coincidently, just a few hours after his death.

Lenny Bruce
(1925–1966)

Abstract: How do you like me now, Honey?
Birth name: Leonard Alfred Schneider
Birthplace: Mineola, New York, USA
Peak Performance: Cafe Au Go Go, Greenwich Village, 1964
Demons: The transition from telling jokes to becoming the punch line

"All my humor is based on destruction and despair."
—**Interview with** *Newsweek*, **1961**

Christians have Jesus. Intellectuals have Socrates. For comedians, the one true martyr is Lenny Bruce, patron saint of stand-up comedy and defender of our constitutional right to talk dirty and influence people. At a time when other comics were milking stale bits about Chinese waiters (with all due respect to Mr. Hackett), Lenny pulled audiences into a world of social satire, scorn for the establishment, and, of course, profanity. And while his legacy will forever be dominated by the obscenity battles that derailed his career, his contribution to the American laughscape did not merely open the floodgates for unchecked foul-mouthery. Lenny's improvisational diatribes on society's ills reimagined what stand-up comedy could be, freeing it from the formulaic setups and corny punch lines that had defined the form.

Lenny was one of the first comics to embrace his tortured psyche. The fact that he was ultimately found naked on the bathroom floor of his Hollywood Hills home, dead of a morphine overdose at the age of forty, mandates his inclusion in any semieclectic anthology of tortured artists. Yet the catalyst behind Lenny's transformation from nightclub obscurity to counterculture hero was not the glut of booze and drugs that led to his untimely demise but rather the broken heart he acquired along the way.

To understand how lovesickness factored into the formation of Lenny's infamous comic persona, it's necessary to go back to the early 1950s, a time when Lenny was an unremarkable workaday comic, steeped in mediocrity. Early in his career, he tended to err toward the conventional, with a flavorless stand-up routine that consisted of little more than innocuous pot shots and the occasional Katharine Hepburn impression. In effect, he played it safe, held back. The manic energy that he would later unleash in a flurry of comic tirades against the established order was, at the time, focused on passions of a

"their relationship was a frenetic one, marked by excessive drug use, wild sex orgies, and the kind of all-night showbiz parties that typically ended with someone getting hit over the head with a hookah pipe"

different sort—namely a beautiful and sexually charged young stripper called Hot Honey Harlow, whom Lenny met in a Baltimore coffee shop in 1951 and married that same year.

Security—especially of the emotional sort—had never been a presence in Lenny's life. His parents divorced when he was five, and he spent much of his childhood getting shuffled between assorted Long Island relatives. His mother, a nightclub performer and aspiring Broadway diva, took him to live with her in Manhattan for a time, but she considered single motherhood a cramp on her glitzy lifestyle. Within months, she shipped Lenny back to the sterile recesses of Nassau County, scarring him with a lifelong case of separation anxiety. Years later, Lenny's impulsive marriage to Honey Harlow offered him the emotional security that was absent from his fractured upbringing.

Lenny and Honey were kindred drifters. They had both run away from home in their teens—he to join the navy and she to dance with a carnival—and they were drawn together by a mutual interest in the bottommost fringes of show business. Their relationship was a frenetic one, marked by excessive drug use, wild sex orgies, and the kind of all-night showbiz parties that typically ended with someone getting hit over the head with a hookah pipe.

From the outset, Lenny was enthralled by Honey's arresting mix of raw sexuality and angelic beauty. He called her a cross between a hooker and the Madonna, the perfect woman to satisfy his need for excitement and security in equal doses. Unfortunately, the fear of abandonment that had latched onto Lenny's psyche from childhood thwarted his chances for a healthy relationship. He was intensely jealous and possessive, and at one point he even insisted that Honey give up stripping because he couldn't bear the thought of other men ogling her. The couple's financial situation was dire, however, and Lenny was not earning enough from his occasional club gigs to support them. Despite his objections, Honey continued to accept stripping jobs whenever she could—out of town, of course, where he couldn't witness the aforementioned ogling. The time apart put a further strain on their relationship until the free-spirited Honey finally decided she could no longer put up with Lenny's fierce possessiveness. The two divorced in January 1957.

With Honey gone and his career still puttering along in first gear, Lenny found himself alone and deeply depressed. Determined not to drown in a pool of self-pity, however, he took his unrequited passion for Honey and channeled it into the one thing he had left: his act. It wasn't long before an edgier comic persona began to emerge. Lenny, as if gerrymandering a new identity out of bitterness and spite, soon perfected the feral voice that would make him both famous and infamous.

Within a year after his breakup, he started to gain a following among late-fifties counterculture types for his outlandish bits on everything from religion to racism to sniffing airplane glue—not to mention his frequent rants on marriage and divorce. Even Honey conceded that his later success might have been the result of her abandonment. "I think Lenny just wanted to show me what I had given up," she admitted in a 1998 documentary. "And he did."

Lenny, as any First Amendment aficionado knows, was not rewarded for the distinctive voice he discovered after his breakup. In 1961, he was charged with obscenity, mainly for saying the word "cocksucker" in a San Francisco nightclub. Although acquitted on that charge, Lenny landed on the radar of morality police across the country. Several more arrests followed, and soon club owners were afraid to book him. In 1964, Lenny's many detractors finally got their way when the comic was convicted of obscenity for two performances at the Cafe Au Go Go in Greenwich Village. Bankrupt and increasingly desperate, Lenny became obsessed with clearing his name, toiling over law journals and preparing for a legal vindication that would never come. He died less than two years later, while the case was still under appeal.

Today, we take George Carlin's "seven dirty words" and *Eddie Murphy Raw* as established watersheds in the annals of American stand-up comedy, but without the obscenity battles fought by Lenny Bruce, contemporary comics might still be subjected to the same draconian censorship imposed upon their predecessors. Larry the Cable Guy aside, the art of making people laugh is far better off without the restraints and forever indebted to Lenny and Honey's irreconcilable differences. ∽

The People vs. Lenny Bruce, a Mini-Timeline

1961—Bruce is arrested after a performance at the Cafe Au Go Go in Greenwich Village.

1964—Bruce is convicted of obscenity, despite a petition signed by Paul Newman, Elizabeth Taylor, Woody Allen, and many others urging that the charges be dropped.

2003—New York Governor George Pataki acknowledges Bruce's invaluable contributions by overturning the comic's obscenity conviction. It was the first posthumous pardon in the state's history.

4

My Way

Control (and the Controlling Control Freaks Who Need It)

The artist as control freak? Thanks to the ubiquity of twenty-first-century media, the tirades of controlling artists are more publicly accessible than ever. Log onto YouTube and you can revisit Christian Bale as he lambastes a cinematographer for ruining a scene or watch David O. Russell and Lily Tomlin lock horns on the set of *I Heart Huckabees*. But tales of headstrong artists jostling for control over their work did not originate in modern-day Hollywood. Consider that, more than a century ago, the Russian playwright Anton Chekhov fought constantly with the famed director Konstantin Stanislavski over the interpretation of his plays. Chekhov saw them as comedies; Stanislavski, as dramas. Often, the former felt his work was mangled beyond recognition. "All I can say is that Stanislavski has wrecked my play," Chekhov said of *The Cherry Orchard*, now among his most cherished masterpieces, when it first opened in 1904. Stanislavski, likewise, had harsh words for Chekhov's ability to play nice, calling him "stern, implacable, and absolutely uncompromising over artistic issues." Theater scholars have since come to appreciate both comedic and dramatic renditions of Chekhov's plays, suggesting that the two men were equally hard headed. But then that's one of the great things about art: It allows us to take pleasure in the creative labors of narrow-minded people whom, in real life, we would probably hate.

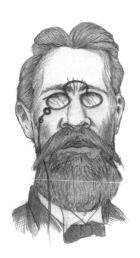

Anton Chekhov

So what happens when tenacity and vision meet obstinacy and arrogance? Frequently, the results can be overindulgent. Give an artist too much creative control, and the next thing you know, *Kill Bill* is two movies. Then again, a controlling presence is not always detrimental to the project at hand. As we'll see with the following case studies, a healthy dose of bull-headedness can go a long way in creating a masterwork—or ten. Only hindsight can tell us if an artist's immutable vision is truly justified, but it's safe to say that any masterpiece worth making requires a strong, if inflexible, personality to see it through.

Michelangelo
(1475–1564)

Abstract: Anything you can do, I can do better
Birth name: Michelangelo di Lodovico Buonarroti Simoni
Birthplace: Caprese, Tuscany, Italy
Masterwork: The ceiling of the Sistine Chapel
Demons: Terminal one-upmanship

"No painting or sculpture will ever quiet my soul."
—**On his final masterpiece,** *The Rondanini Pietà,* **circa 1556**

"When I returned to Florence, I found myself famous," Michelangelo Buonarroti boasted in a diary entry, recalling the summer of 1501, when he arrived back in his adopted hometown after a successful five-year stint in Rome. He had a reason to feel cocky that year. At twenty-six, he had just completed work on a stunning new marble statue called the *Pietà.* The piece, depicting the freshly crucified body of Jesus cradled in his mother's lap, was commissioned by the French Cardinal Jean de Billheres. It was no small achievement for a young artist from humble origins, the son of a small-town government official. Garnering ample acclaim throughout the region, the statue helped solidify Michelangelo's reputation as the hottest sculptor in Italy. This kid was going places, and he knew it.

Michelangelo's superb abilities were generating a buzz, all right, but then so was his predilection for egomaniacal behavior, which was rapidly becoming infamous within artistic and political circles. Word on the street was that you could just not work with the guy. He was rude, quick tempered, and downright unprofessional.

Even the warmongering Pope Julius II, Michelangelo's largest patron, had trouble getting the artist to meet deadlines and contractual obligations. "You can do nothing with him!" His Holiness once griped.

As it happens, many of Michelangelo's antisocial work habits stemmed from the fact that he was fiercely competitive with other artists. He refused to work with collaborators or apprentices, preferring instead to chisel in solitude. Shortly after the *Pietà* was completed, he overheard a comment by one of the Roman locals who believed the statue had been carved by a rival sculptor named Cristoforo Solari. In a fit of rage, Michelangelo, late one night, broke into the mausoleum where the statue was displayed and chiseled the unambiguous inscription, "Michelangelo Buonarroti, Florentine, made this." Such behavior was not typically tolerated from sculptors at a time when they were considered little more than skilled laborers, but Michelangelo received more leniency than most. He was just that talented.

And yet, for all his abilities, Michelangelo still harbored the private pangs of a man who secretly felt inadequate alongside artists with more diverse achievements. As a sculptor

"he was rude, quick tempered, and downright unprofessional"

Michelangelo was unmatched, praised the world over for the *Pietà* and later the statue of *David*. As a painter, however, he was far less proficient. And that lack of diversity put him in the shadow of older, more accomplished Renaissance men, particularly Leonardo da Vinci, a revered master of painting, sculpture, music, science, engineering, and pretty much everything else. In modern context, Michelangelo might seem a raving one-upman, a Gladwellian outlier determined to be the best at everything he tried. Back then, people probably just thought he was a self-absorbed jerk. Either way, he was ruefully tortured by the fact that artists such as Leonardo had skills that surpassed his own. In fact, it was this voracious desire for unmatched greatness that drove the creation of his most enduring masterpiece, a work that stands today as one of the defining achievements of the High Renaissance—the ceiling frescoes of the Sistine Chapel.

In 1508, Michelangelo was summoned back to Rome by Pope Julius II, who wanted to hire him for the ambitious paintings that would span the chapel ceiling. The sculptor had no experience in fresco; indeed, he had barely worked with color at all. So why would the pope entrust him with such a high-profile project—on a ceiling, no less? For that curious honor, Michelangelo could once again blame his inability to work with others. As it turns out, his Sistine Chapel gig was a setup, a scheme to ruin his reputation. The architect Donato Bramante, a colleague who had grown tired of working with the ornery artist, personally persuaded Julius II to give Michelangelo the job of the chapel ceiling. Bramante believed that Michelangelo would either turn it down or simply botch it to the point of embarrassment. What he did not count on, however, was Michelangelo's burning need to prove himself as the world's greatest living artist—a title he knew he could not earn without broadening his talents. He took the large-scale Sistine Chapel job knowing it would establish him as every bit the painter as he was a sculptor.

Of course, Michelangelo wasted no time commandeering the project in true Michelangelo style. Within a year, he fired most of his assistants and told the pontiff that he wanted more creative control. The pope grew impatient, as popes do, but Michelangelo could not resist getting carried away, taking the original plan from grand to grandiose. The result is a vast and intricate arrangement of biblical scenes, including the famous *Creation of Adam*, in which the whiskered almighty, looking like Willie Nelson on steroids, touches fingers with the first man on Earth.

The Sistine Chapel opened to the public on October 31, 1512, and Julius II died less than four months later. When it was all over, Michelangelo was nearly dead himself. He later complained of the "four tortured years" that took their toll on his body. Still, the project gave him the chance to finally prove his diversity, and as the years progressed he grew even more diverse, accomplishing feats in engineering, architecture, even poetry. Through it all, though, his obsession with his own greatness never left his mind, even as it became clear that his best years were passing him by. Mortality did not sit well with Michelangelo. The man who celebrated male potency in *David* grew repulsed by his aging body. He spoke of his wrinkled face, his loose teeth, and the ringing in his ears as if they were some kind of debt for his former artistic prowess. "This is the state where art has led me, after granting me glory," he said in his final years. "Poor, old, beaten, I will be reduced to nothing if death does not come swiftly to my rescue."

Clash of the Titans

In 1504, Michelangelo was commissioned to paint a mural in the Great Council Hall of Florence's Palazzo Vecchio. It was a terrific honor—a battle monument to celebrate the newly reinstated Florentine republic. There was just one small problem: Leonardo da Vinci, Michelangelo's greatest rival, was commissioned to paint a different mural in the same room. Now, the two men would have to work side by side, in competition, as onlookers compared and judged their respective murals. It was the paint-off of the century, an event that drew spectators from around the world. Unfortunately for anyone who expected a Herculean sporting event, the competition ended anticlimactically, cut short by the fact that Michelangelo and Leonardo, their differences notwithstanding, shared a gross tendency to procrastinate. Both artists failed to complete their murals before eventually getting roped into other projects. When the republic fell in 1512, funding for the murals fell with it.

There is something paradoxical in the thought of Michelangelo, the immortal artist, waiting around for death. One could argue that he's still waiting. Five hundred years after it was painted, the ceiling of the Sistine Chapel still attracts some 4 million visitors every year. Even for the most restless of egos, that's a nice little stroke. ∾

Maria Callas
(1923–1977)

Abstract: It's not over until the skinny girl sings
Birth name: Maria Anna Sophia Cecilia Kalogeropoulou
Birthplace: New York, New York, USA
Peak Performance: In the title role of *La Gioconda,* Verona Arena, 1947
Demons: Carbs

"I was the ugly duckling, fat and clumsy and unpopular."
—Interview with *Time* magazine, 1956

When dissecting the fractured and frenzied life of the legendary opera singer Maria Callas, two points must be made clear. First, the widely reported rumor that she deliberately swallowed a tapeworm to lose weight is probably untrue. Second, just because she didn't deliberately swallow a tapeworm doesn't mean she wasn't crazy enough to do it. And yet if reports of her weight-loss methods were overblown, then her reputation for temper tantrums, vicious rivalries, familial discord, and failed love affairs is well earned.

Callas's status as the quintessential diva remains unchallenged, even by Mariah Carey's ever-increasing list of backstage demands.

The famed dramatic soprano went from stout to svelte and became the transformative prima donna of the opera world, a furniture-throwing, litigation-happy starlet who made headlines wherever she went.

None of this is to suggest that Callas's overt diva demeanor was not backed up by serious talent. (Pay attention, Mariah.) The extraordinary range of her voice gained her an audience of staunch devotees almost immediately following her debut in 1947, when she performed in Ponchielli's *La Gioconda* at Italy's Verona Arena. To be sure, her voice was an imperfect one, fraught with hollowness and shrills but buoyed by powerful and expressive performances. Her vivid interpretations of the roles she played made her unique at a time when other opera singers did little more than stand around and wear Viking hats. By 1953, Maria was a star. But she was larger than life in more ways than one.

Weight had always been an embarrassing issue for Maria, from her childhood in upper Manhattan through her adolescence in Athens. A rotund frump of a child, she grew up in the shadow of an outgoing and slender older sister, whom her mother groomed for marriage to the wealthiest husband she could find. For Maria, she had other plans. After rec-

"her reputation for temper tantrums, vicious rivalries, familial discord, and failed love affairs is well earned"

ognizing the outstanding singing ability of her younger daughter, Maria's mother hoped to keep the girl as she was, plump and awkward, so that her potential singing career would not be thwarted by the likes of a gentleman suitor. Not that suitors would be a problem. Maria spent her adolescence in a veritable social coma, watching handsome men eat out of her sister's hand while she stayed at home binging on fatty Greek dishes and feeling repulsive to the opposite sex. To make matters worse, she apparently didn't smell any better than she looked. Her skin was allergic to perfumes and deodorants, which made summers in Athens a particularly putrid ordeal. However, if her appearance damaged her sense of self-worth within social circles, she soon discovered her source of confidence through her tremendous voice, which earned her not only praise and admiration but also scholarships to Athenian music conservatories. When Maria's mother urged her young daughter to pursue opera as a career, Maria agreed, but only on the condition that she one day become a "great singer." By the time she began her vocal training, she was already declaring her ambition to perform in the world's greatest opera houses. Not everyone believed she could achieve this goal, of course. Maria's first teacher took one look at her round, pimply face, thick-rimmed glasses, and gnarled fingernails and dismissed her ambitions as "laughable." But Maria did not let herself be deterred. If she could not control her weight, she could still control her destiny.

This brings us back to 1953. Maria was at the top of her game, having appeared at nearly every major opera house in Italy, but the food-loving soprano had still not conquered her greatest vice. She was pushing 200 pounds, and the gossipy magpies of the Italian opera world were starting to talk. One critic, reviewing her performance in Verdi's *Aida*, joked that he could not tell Maria's chunky legs from those of the elephant in the scene with her. The review brought Maria to bitter tears, but soon she would vow to make them all eat their hearts out.

It was when a director gave Maria an ultimatum—lose weight or else—that she finally realized enough was enough. Over the next year, Maria's weight loss was dramatic and rapid, fueling endless speculation about how she pulled it off, including the aforementioned tapeworm rumor. The singer was, in fact, treated for tapeworms, but the worms were likely the result of her fondness for raw steak, not because she had deliberately swallowed them to shed pounds. The real story behind her methods, however, is no less bizarre. Enlisting a group of Swiss doctors, she underwent a dangerous treatment whereby she was administered large doses of thyroid extract to increase her metabolism. When that proved to be too slow a method, she had iodine applied directly to her thyroid, which melted pounds quickly but also wreaked havoc on her nervous system.

Nevertheless, by 1954, Maria had emerged the very image of beauty and glamour, captivating audiences with her newly sculpted features, intense dark eyes, and trim figure. Her elephantine legs had given way to slight calves and delicate ankles, tapered off by high-heeled shoes instead of the clumpy Oxfords she used to wear. And as she transformed, so did her wardrobe, with Europe's top designers offering her chic gowns to wear at public functions. Maria Callas, the frumpy fat lady of opera, had enacted her revenge by becoming the very symbol of Parisian and Milanese elegance.

In the end, however, the change was less a butterfly-like transformation than a Faustian bargain, and her tiny new frame seemed to come with the ultimate price: the diminished power of her voice. Indeed, many of those who followed her career felt that, after 1955, Maria's vocal ability was never the same. "When she lost the weight, she couldn't seem to sustain the great sound that she had made," said fellow soprano Joan Sutherland in a BBC interview. "The body seemed to be too frail." With her voice in continual decline, Maria's singing career was essentially over by her

It's All a Blur

Stage fright crippled Maria Callas's performances in her early years, almost derailing her career before it started. Fortunately, she was blessed by one particular malady that helped her overcome her intense fear of performing: myopia. Severely nearsighted since childhood, Maria wore thick-lens glasses throughout her vocal training. But when she took them off, audience members became faceless blurs. No longer inhibited by the critical facial expressions of opera crowds, Maria was free to unleash the voice that would come to be known as "that voice."

early forties, but her metamorphosis continues to fascinate anyone who enjoys a good duckling-to-swan fable with a bastardized twist. Since her death in 1977, countless biographies have been written about her, and she remains one of the top-selling opera artists of all time. Maria Callas may have traded talent for looks, but at least she got a legacy out of the bargain. Faust just went to hell. ∼

Walt Disney
(1901–1966)

Abstract: Revenge is a talking rodent wearing pants
Birth name: Walter Elias Disney
Birthplace: Chicago, Illinois, USA
Masterwork: *Steamboat Willie*
Demons: The knife in his back

"Born of necessity, the little fellow literally freed us of immediate worry."

—On creating Mickey Mouse, attributed via the Walt Disney World Resort

The name Disney is synonymous with everything from family-friendly cartoons to sunny Florida vacations to the insidious homogenization of virtually every form of entertainment. Yet the namesake behind these larger-than-life manifestations was an unassuming midwestern cartoonist who would famously remind his awestruck admirers, "It all started with a mouse." Walt Disney's totemic rodent is easily among the world's most recognizable symbols—right up there with the crucifix, the Buddha, and the Starbucks siren. However, it may surprise many Disneyphiles to learn that it wasn't kind-heartedness and warm fuzzies that led to Mickey Mouse's creation; it was good-old-fashioned anger and scorn.

Back in his pre-Mickey days, circa 1927, the young Walt Disney had already made a modest name for himself in animation circles with a cartoon critter named Oswald the Lucky Rabbit, whom he created with the help of his partner, Ub Iwerks. Oswald's growing popularity prompted Walt to ask his boss for a pay raise. However, the young animator was taken aback when said boss, producer Charles B. Mintz, told Walt his salary was actually being *decreased* in an effort to cut skyrocketing overhead. When Walt refused to accept the pay cut, Mintz cut him loose and stole his entire team of animators in the process—except for Iwerks, who loyally remained at Walt's side. Walt lost the rights to Oswald the Lucky Rabbit, who was owned by a fledgling little film outfit known as Universal Studios. Walt Disney was shocked by the betrayal and downright infuriated by the loss of his favorite character.

The young artist, who was as naive as he was stubborn, couldn't fathom how his coworkers could so easily turn against him. Nevertheless, he vowed to bounce back, and soon he and Iwerks began to collaborate on a new character—one based on a real-life rodent that Walt would sometimes feed at his original Kansas City studio. That character became Mickey

"it wasn't kindheartedness and warm fuzzies that led to Mickey Mouse's creation; it was good-old-fashioned anger and scorn"

Mouse, who in turn became a sensation in November 1928 with his third film, *Steamboat Willie*, which was billed as the first cartoon talkie.

The experience of being stabbed in the back not only sparked the creation of Walt's most beloved character but also the multimedia empire that remains his legacy. Upon Mickey's success, every studio in town, including Walt's former employer Universal Studios, was clamoring to sign the pioneering animator behind the magic. The problem? Every studio in town also insisted on retaining the rights to Mickey Mouse as part of a distribution deal. This was one concession Walt refused to make, and he opted instead to use Mickey's success to further the reach of his own company. It didn't matter that his company at the time comprised only three employees. Having learned his lesson from the Oswald treachery, Walt Disney made sure he retained control over everything created under the Disney name from then on. Five movie studios, seven theme parks, and six Broadway juggernauts later, it's safe to say his control-freak tendencies paid off. ∽

The Empire Strikes Back

In 2006, The Walt Disney Company bought the rights to Oswald the Lucky Rabbit from NBC Universal. The move came forty years after Walt Disney's death and seventy-eight years after he originally lost the character to Universal and producer Charles Mintz in a bitter power struggle. Rest in peace, Walt.

Madonna
(b. 1958)

Abstract: Frailness is not an option
Birth name: Madonna Louise Ciccone
Birthplace: Bay City, Michigan, USA
Peak Performance: Singing "Like a Virgin" atop a giant wedding cake at the first-ever MTV Video Music Awards, 1984
Demons: A frustrating inability to rule the universe

"I became an overachiever to get approval from the world."
—**Interview with *Spin* magazine, 1996**

In the fickle world of pop music, where it's better to burn out than fade away, Madonna has done neither. Her enduring, dance-friendly anthems exploded from the East Village club scene to become the signature sound of the 1980s and a staple of Nina Blackwood–era MTV. Her early fashion, an amalgam of thrift-store chic and post-punk frills, emerged as the default look for a generation of teen girls determined to fit as many jelly bracelets onto one arm as possible. And while a lesser artist might have been content with defining the sound and style of an entire decade, Madonna brazenly retooled her image time and again to ensure her relevance. She channeled Marilyn Monroe as the Material Girl. She spoofed Fritz Lang in *Express Yourself*. She infiltrated late-nineties raves with *Ray of Light*. What's more, she did it all while maintaining a decades-long movie career, despite repeated pleas from Roger Ebert that she stick to music. Though her reputation for commercial shrewdness is well deserved, the true force behind Madonna's success is a far more visceral animal: a need for power and control set into motion by a traumatic loss she suffered while growing up in small-town life in Michigan.

In 1962, Madonna's mother, pregnant with her sixth child, was diagnosed with breast cancer—an apparent consequence of working as an x-ray technician before protective aprons were made mandatory. She delayed treatment until her baby was born, but by that time it was too late. A harrowing, yearlong battle with the disease ensued.

Madonna, then a fiery five year old whose need for the spotlight had already begun to surface, was at first confused and maddened by her mother's waning health.

"Madonna spent her formative years haunted by memories of a frail and dying mother"

The pop star would later recall the dread she felt upon discovering how physically weak her mother had become. For the Material Girl in training, it was a defining moment, one that triggered a lifelong fear of powerlessness. "I knew I could either be sad and weak and not in control, or I could just take control and say it's going to get better," she told *Time* magazine in 1985.

Madonna spent her formative years haunted by memories of a frail and dying mother, building the ambition that would assure her success in all things. However, this overachieving fervor might never have found its true constructive purpose if not for a second childhood trauma.

In 1966, Madonna's father, Tony Ciccone, married the family housekeeper, Joan. Since her mother's death three years earlier,

Madonna, now eight and increasingly headstrong, had formed an unusually strong attachment to her father, and she saw his second marriage as a betrayal. Joan's entrance into the Ciccone family ignited a rebellious streak in Madonna that would punctuate her adolescence and, later, her career. The two of them, equally stubborn, played out a sort of Cinderella/Wicked Stepmother relationship, nettled by Madonna's burgeoning need to push the boundaries of what she could say, what she could wear, and whom she could date—three facets of her life that would later make her a tabloid favorite. This bitter stepmother-daughter conflict finally came to a boil in 1978 when Madonna dropped out of the University of Michigan, where she had been attending on a dance scholarship, and left home for New York City, determined to set the world ablaze and claim her crown.

There is no denying that Madonna achieved pop-music royalty. Even her cheeky tabloid designation, Madge, is British shorthand for Your Majesty. However, she likely never would have been appointed to the court had it not been for years of childhood distress. We can only assume her early trauma was far more tormenting than anything she would experience later in life (with the possible exception of suffering through the reviews for *Swept Away*), but thankfully these experiences equipped her with the tools to enact change as she saw fit. More than a nonconformist, Madonna is one of those rare artists who forced the world to conform to her: hence the skirt-over-Capri-pants look, which is still acceptable to this day. ⌒

J. K. Rowling
(b. 1965)

Abstract: The wizard of id
Birth name: Joanne Rowling
Birthplace: Yate, Gloucestershire, England
Masterwork: The *Harry Potter* series
Demons: Mortality

"No magic power can resurrect a truly dead person."
—Interview with the *Guardian,* 2000

Much has been written about J. K. Rowling's rapid transformation from state-assisted single mother to modern-day mythmaker. The deceptively humble wordsmith behind the boy wizard Harry Potter not only unleashed the most wide-reaching pop-culture phenomenon of the last fifteen years but also went on to become the first billion-dollar book author on the planet. Not bad for a former English teacher who wrote most of her debut novel in longhand at a tiny Edinburgh café during her baby daughter's naptime. In those days, Joanne Rowling, or Jo, was still in shock from having hit rock bottom. She was unemployed, recently divorced, and struggling to support her only child on a meager seventy pounds a week. "I was the biggest failure I knew," she said. But failure was liberating to the young writer, a means of "stripping away the inessential" and focusing solely on her craft.

In regard to her standing as a tortured artist, Jo Rowling might seem a tad too optimistic to wear the title—a resourceful coper who resolved cheerfully to shrug off poverty and finish her labor of love. And yet behind her determined exterior lies a lonely pain, one that festered in Jo's psyche throughout her adolescence. On the eve of Harry's birth, it exploded, only to become the very thing that gave him his soul.

In 1990, on a delayed train from Manchester to London, the idea of a black-haired boy who learns he's a wizard first popped into Jo's head. She was not carrying a pen at the time, and being shy around strangers, she could not bring herself to ask for one. Instead, the twenty-five year old sat silently among the other commuters, dreaming up the various characters and creatures that she thought might inhabit her wizard's fanciful universe. That night she eagerly began writing what would become *Harry Potter and the Philosopher's Stone*, the first in the seven-book series, but those first few pages bore little resemblance to the capacious and clear-minded allegory that would one day cast a spell over Millennials the world over. Jo's story needed focus; her fertile imagination was pulling her in too many directions. Even more frustrating was the fact that her story arc lacked a singular theme—something both universal and grand to infuse the ambitious concept with the import it deserved. It wouldn't be long, however, before the thematic world of Harry Potter would become tragically cemented by the news that Jo's

> "she was unemployed, recently divorced, and struggling to support her only child on a meager seventy pounds a week"

mother, Anne, lost her ten-year battle with multiple sclerosis. It was the most devastating shock of Jo's life.

It's not that Jo had been oblivious to her mother's failing health. Since the age of fifteen, she had watched helplessly as Anne gradually lost her ability to perform everyday tasks, her body rebelling against itself in disrepair. But Jo had somehow managed to convince herself that the condition was not as serious as it appeared. The girl who would one day conjure up Quidditch games and cauldron cakes had such an inherent knack for fantasy that her instinct was to deny the inconceivable reality. Death, while imminent, was simply too painful to consider. "I don't know how I didn't realize how ill she was," she said in an interview, recalling the last time she'd seen Anne alive, thin and exhausted. It was during that final visit that Jo adopted her now-famous tight-lipped policy in regard to projects in development. She never told her mother about the fantastic idea gestating in her head, the wizard named Harry who at the time was nothing more than a scrawl of notes. Soon it would be too late. Anne passed away in December 1990, only a few months after Harry's conception. The death of Jo Rowling's mother unleashed nascent controlling tendencies buried within Jo's emotional interior.

Like Madonna, whose own mother's death filled her with a lifelong fear of powerlessness, Jo became overwhelmed by the realization that fate can deal us a fatal blow at any time. Yet the ways in which these two artists fed their quests for control could not have been more different. The material girl, as we recall, fled to New York and set out to dominate the material world. But Jo turned her pursuits inward, tunneling ever deeper into a universe populated by witches, warlocks, and the occasional house elf. In the real world, Jo was a powerless Muggle who could do nothing as her mother succumbed to an insidious disease. In the imaginary world of Harry Potter, however, there were no limits to Jo's power, and the writer gave herself carte blanche to fashion a reality that suited her. It was her creation, governed by her logic.

Peppered liberally throughout the Potterverse is constant evidence of Jo's pain and isolation. (Consider the Dementors, the soul-sucking fiends that feed on human happiness, inspired by Jo's draining bout with clinical depression.) Yet despite the magic and fantasy of Harry's reality, Jo saddled her creation with one sobering truth that mirrors our own: The characters, be they warlocks, wizards, or what have you, cannot cheat death. "Once you're dead you're dead," she said bluntly of her characters' mortality.

As death emerged as the chief theme of the *Harry Potter* series, it became keenly reflected in the life of its bespectacled protagonist. As a baby, Harry's parents are murdered by the evil Voldemort, a Dark Lord whose obsession with immortality is shared by the author herself. "I so understand why Voldemort wants to conquer death," she admitted. "We're all frightened of it."

The death of J. K. Rowling's mother took place just as her daughter's greatest creation was being born. The weight of that tragedy fed the inventive young writer an unkind dose of reality, one that elevated her whimsical tale of a boy wizard by grounding it in the deepest fears of us earthbound humans. ∼

Women's Writes

The publishing industry has apparently not abandoned its long and tiring history of hiding the gender of female writers. In 1997, when the first *Harry Potter* book was nearing publication, Rowling's British publisher, Bloomsbury, rightly believed that young boys would make up a sizable segment of Harry's audience. Not wanting to alienate that demographic, Bloomsbury asked Rowling to dump her first name in lieu of two initials. Rowling, who has no middle name, picked "K" as her second initial, after her grandmother Kathleen. Her unisex byline puts her in the company of countless female authors, including—to name a few—Charlotte Brontë, who published *Jane Eyre* under the gender-neutral name Currer Bell, and Mary Shelley, who published *Frankenstein* anonymously. Perhaps the most obvious Rowling comparison is Susan Eloise Hinton, whose publisher urged her to use her initials out of fear of alienating a presumably male audience for her debut novel, *The Outsiders*.

James Cameron
(b. 1954)

Abstract: Opening Pandora's box
Birth name: James Francis Cameron
Birthplace: Kapuskasing, Ontario, Canada
Masterwork: *Avatar*
Demons: Idleness

"There are going to be little windows of opportunity that open for a split second, and you either squirt through or you don't."
—**Interview with the Academy of Achievement, 1999**

For irrefutable evidence of our one-time willingness to overlook cheesy special effects, consider *Logan's Run*, the 1976 film that takes plastic egg cartons and tries to pass them off as an advanced bubble city of the twenty-third century. That the film earned an Academy Award for its visual efforts says less about its ability to blow the minds of seventies moviegoers and more about the fact that Hollywood, in those days, simply had nothing better to offer.

James Cameron, a young truck driver and community college dropout living in Southern California, thought he could do better, although he had no idea how he might pull it off. He spent much of his spare time scribbling down ideas for stories set on alien worlds and in distant galaxies—ideas that Hollywood had yet to effectively conceptualize—but in reality he was just another no-name kid with a drawer full of unfinished scripts.

Then, in the summer of 1977, James went to see a sci-fi adventure movie called *Star Wars*, and as he watched the film's fantastic space battles unfold on screen, a wave of humility choked him. When it was over, he was left with a maddening realization: This was the movie he should have made. He had spent years passively dreaming up stories in his head while a fellow Southern Californian named George Lucas—only ten years his senior—went out and created a groundbreaking achievement in visual effects. (Watch *Star Wars* next to *Logan's Run*, and you will not believe that the two films were released only a year apart.) James left the theater that day in a fury of self-defeat, wounded by the knowledge that great ideas will not wait around for languid gestation.

That summer, as the entire country got swept up in *Star Wars* mania, James got swept up in his own anger. He became obsessed with figuring out exactly how Lucas brought *Star Wars* to the screen. He spent his spare time at the campus library of the University of Southern California, Lucas's alma mater, where he would pore through thesis papers on special effects, front-screen projection, optical printing—anything he could find. He bought some cheap film equipment and started teaching himself how to use a camera. Teaming up with a friend, James wrote a screenplay for a space-age movie called *Xenogenesis*, and he managed to raise $20,000 to produce a twelve-minute segment from the film. James chose to film one of the script's key scenes, which featured a battle between a giant robot and a woman wearing an exoskeleton. Employing his OCD-like eye for detail, he spent countless hours crafting the two miniature models he needed for the fight scene, and then he used stop-motion animation to bring the sequence to life.

When it was all finished, James hawked the segment to various Hollywood studios, hoping to convince someone to produce the full film. Unfortunately, his pitch had become all too familiar. Although California's 1978 census report does not specify how many budding filmmakers went around that year claiming they could make the next *Star Wars*, James was certainly not alone. But while *Xenogenesis* did not land him a movie deal, his miniature models did catch the eye of Roger Corman, the consummate B-movie crackerjack, who hired James to build model spaceships for his 1980 sci-fi spectacle, *Battle Beyond the Stars*. From there James worked his way up the chain of visual-effects specialists until finally getting the chance to direct the film *Piranha II: The Spawning*. Granted, it was a low-budget camp fest about flying fish that eat human flesh, but James deftly parlayed it into an opportunity to direct a creation of his own conceiving, a film about a cyborg assassin sent back in time to kill the mother of his enemy. The enormous success of that film, *The Terminator*, made James a sought-after sci-fi director. He was no George Lucas, but he was on his way.

James's fixation on minute details and technological envelope pushing became a signature trait, propelling not only his own directorial efforts but the special-effects industry as a whole. For *The Terminator* sequel, released in 1991, he employed then-unproven computer-animation techniques to create a shape-shifting assassin made out of liquid metal. The effects are not exactly eye

> **"a creation of his own conceiving, a film about a cyborg assassin sent back in time to kill the mother of his enemy"**

candy by today's standards, but they set the stage for modern computer-generated spectacles and, in an ironic twist, helped turn model making into a lost art. As James's Hollywood dominance grew, so too did his obsession with technical perfection, which almost ended his reign.

In early 1997, when he was waist deep in production for *Titanic*, Hollywood was abuzz with talk of his downfall. His film was months behind schedule; it was a hundred million dollars over budget, and James was gaining a bad reputation for his dictatorial directing methods, which had him flying over *Titanic*'s massive sets in a crane, chewing out crewmembers with a bullhorn.

His obsession meant that by the time his film *Titanic* was released, James had spent an unprecedented $200 million on a three-hour movie that everyone already knew the ending to. *Titanic* was expected to sink faster than its eponymous ship, and James was expected to get sucked under right along with it. Of course, both proved unsinkable.

Titanic became the top-earning movie of all time, a spot it held for twelve years before it was finally toppled by another James Cameron movie. It was shortly after the release of *Titanic* that James conceived of a story set on a distant moon inhabited by giant blue aliens. Gone were the days when his ideas would have to collect dust in a drawer, but this time something else was standing in his way: The technology needed to film the movie did not exist yet. And just as he once spent hours building miniature models for a twelve-minute sequence, he would now spend his time developing a new camera for motion-capture animation. The result was *Avatar*, a 3D sci-fi fantasy that became the first movie in history to gross more than $2 billion. Monetary considerations aside, *Avatar* stands out for another reason: It's one of the few films of the last decade to reach bona fide blockbuster status without the benefit of a previous tie in. In an industry that now subsists almost entirely on the recycled lifeblood of familiar superheroes and old TV shows, James's blue-alien universe brings something fresh to the pop-culture pantheon. It's too early to predict if his creation will have enough longevity to fuel retro treadmills of the future, but there are already two sequels in the works, and clearly

Mr. Cameron will not be happy until the moon-dwelling Na'vi make a lasting impact on the mass consciousness. In interviews, he has indicated his hope that *Avatar* will one day exert a larger cultural influence than, say, the *Star Wars* franchise. It always seems to come back to beating George Lucas. ～

5

Rage Against the Machine

How I Learned to Stop Worrying and Blame Society

Societies, like people, are predictably resistant to change. Complain as we will about oppressive governments, myopic leaders, and draconian penalties, most of us opt for the status quo more often than not. The unknown is a frightening thing, after all, and while society may not be perfect, at least we know what to expect from it.

Sometimes it takes the radical ideas of an artist to kick complacent societies where they need to be kicked. The problem is, societies usually kick back—hard. When artists find themselves fighting against the cultural mores into which they're born, the end results can be at best dangerous and at worst fatal. And yet, rarely does any society succeed in permanently eradicating the ideas it wishes to suppress. Not even Napoleon could do that in 1801, when he ordered his bayonet-wielding cronies to find, and arrest, the anonymous author of sexually explicit books that were circulating around France at the time. That author, it turned out, was the Marquis de Sade, who was caught, arrested, and tossed into a mental asylum. Although Sade was institutionalized for the rest of his life, his work survived. Walk into any bookstore today, and you can pick up a copy of Sade's formerly banned books, and no, the Barnes & Noble security guards will not tackle you on the way out.

Often, artists battle society in ways that are less direct, presenting their controversial ideas in a manner so cryptic that only folks in the know are likely to get the message. In the uptight 1950s, the television writer Rod Serling wanted to challenge viewers with provocative programming, but he grew increasingly frustrated with his craft after endless fights with network censors, who deemed anything outside of *Leave It to Beaver* as too risqué for TV. (In two separate instances, Serling tried to dramatize the harrowing story of Emmett Till, the fourteen-year-old African-American boy who was lynched in Mississippi in 1955. The writer met with censorship both times.) That's when Rod decided that if he had any chance of tackling important issues, he would have to sneak those issues right over the heads of the bromidic decision makers who were axing his material. *The Twilight Zone*, Serling's masterpiece of morality, premiered in 1959, confronting society's ills in a way that television had never before seen. Shielded by the guise of model spaceships, cheap alien makeup, and fake robots, Serling was free to crank out unflinching fables on greed,

racism, mental illness, totalitarianism, and, of course, unchecked censorship.

The following tortured artists fought their own battles against society. The fact that we're still talking about these artists can only mean that their fights ended in victory, although the tragic details of those fights might suggest otherwise.

Rod Serling

Edgar Allan Poe
(1809–1849)

Abstract: The would-be sellout
Birth name: Edgar Poe
Birthplace: Boston, Massachusetts, USA
Masterwork: "The Raven"
Demons: Being devalued

"When shall the artist assume his proper situation in society—in a society of thinking beings? How long shall he be enslaved?"
—*Southern Literary Messenger*, 1836

"Men have called me mad," wrote Edgar Allan Poe in the autobiographical short story "Eleonora," "but the question is not yet settled, whether madness is or is not the loftiest intelligence." It's easy for modern readers to conclude that the question to which Poe referred was settled on October 3, 1849—the day the author was found stumbling aimlessly through the streets of Baltimore, delirious and incoherent, wearing someone else's soiled clothes. That he succumbed to a mysterious illness four days later, following a lifelong battle with addiction and depression, seems to all but cinch the case against madness as a form of lofty intelligence, and the fact that literary scholars and blue-haired Goths still ponder the symbolism behind "The Raven" a century and a half later doesn't really prove otherwise.

The truth is, even in the 1800s, people loved a good story about the connection between creativity and madness, and Poe, one of the original tortured authors of American literature, did not fail to beguile a tragedy-loving public. He was orphaned at the age of two, stricken by the gambling bug in his teens, and drinking heavily by twenty. At twenty-seven, he married the love of his life, who also happened to be his thirteen-year-old cousin, and he later watched her suffer for five years before she finally succumbed to tuberculosis, at the age of twenty-four.

And yet, despite Edgar's unmistakable tortured credentials, he was driven to write by a far more down-to-earth idea—the idea that he could actually earn a living as a writer of fiction and poetry. It's a simple enough concept but quite radical for the 1830s. Back then, American literature was largely printed in weekly and monthly periodicals, the publishers of which stacked the deck firmly in their own favor. They paid low rates, offered no royalties, reprinted stories at their discretion, and often forced writers to use pseudonyms as a means of keeping them anonymous. American magazine publishers often would not pay for new content at all. Rather, they would simply reprint stories by British authors, who, in the absence of international copyright law, had no legal means to stop them. Edgar condemned these nineteenth-century aggregators, decrying their practices as literary piracy. American writers, he believed, did not stand a chance as

> "the author was found stumbling aimlessly through the streets of Baltimore, delirious and incoherent, wearing someone else's soiled clothes"

long as magazines could reprint British stories without paying for them. "Literature is at a sad discount," he bemoaned. "Without an international copyright law, American authors may as well cut their throats."

Nevertheless, Edgar spent his entire adult life trying to profit from his poetry and fiction. Working day jobs at various publications in Richmond, Philadelphia, and New York, he mostly earned his keep as a literary critic or an editor. However, the intermittent employment kept him at best solvent and at worst begging his friends and family for money. If the average tortured writer is obsessed with artistry and unconcerned with monetary compensation, then Edgar was not average.

Indeed, by the time he reached his mid-thirties, he had become so fed up with just scraping by that he set out to write something that would change his fortunes—something specifically meant to appeal to the tastes of both critics and the reading public. The result was a gothic poem about bereavement and a talking raven. The doleful tale was, at least partially, based on Poe's own experience (as the story goes, his young wife, Virginia, was gravely ill while he was working on it), but its depiction of a grieving narrator who is visited in the night by the titular bird was largely an attempt to wow the masses. Consider that the popular writer Charles Dickens, just a few years earlier, had also employed the use of a talking raven in *Barnaby Rudge*.

Nevertheless, "The Raven," upon its publication in 1845, made Edgar an instant celebrity. Critics were not universally kind to its elegiac playfulness, but readers ate it up like so much Halloween candy. Buried within its metrical cadence, the poem captured something universal about the nature of grief—our desire to remember versus our need to forget. Edgar's narrator is torn between them, and mourning for his beloved Lenore becomes a kind of perverse pleasure in itself. Equally responsible for the success of "The Raven" was

Edgar's own poetically tortured backstory: the heavy-drinking gambler, preoccupied with the macabre, whose droopy eyes and upturned brow conveyed the sadness of an abused puppy dog. Women lined up at Edgar's door, vowing to cure him of his self-destructive behavior. Children would chase him down the street, hounding him relentlessly until he turned around, raised his arms, and screeched "Nevermore!" like the titular bird of his poem.

Edgar was thrilled with his newfound fame, but in the absence of compensation to match his renown, he remained little more than a morbid curiosity, a reality star before such things existed. Poor payment was always a point of fierce contention for Edgar, who remained steadfast in his belief that literature doesn't just have meaning; it has value. "I have made no money," Edgar complained after "The Raven" had run its course. "I am as poor now as ever I was in my life—except in hope, which is by no means bankable." A few years later, amid circumstances that still remain a mystery, Edgar somehow got sidetracked on a trip from Richmond to Philadelphia, and he wound up on that fateful Baltimore street, semiconscious. Edgar Allan Poe once called literature "the noblest of professions," but the world he lived in showed him otherwise. The international copyright law that he thought so vital to the future of literature would not be adopted by Congress until 1891, more than four decades after his death. And yet his conviction in its importance was quickly validated by the speed with which the conditions for American writers improved. By the early 1900s, hit novels like Edith Wharton's *The House of Mirth* and Hemingway's *The Sun Also Rises* were generating small fortunes for the authors who penned them.

Today, battles over intellectual property rights have been refashioned for the digital age, with legions of unpaid bloggers weighing their desire for exposure against their need to earn a living. And yet, with its widespread aggregation, the Internet is not all that different from those pilfering periodicals of the nineteenth century. Couldn't you just see Poe toiling away, thanklessly, as a hired gun for *The Huffington Post*? Chances are, he would feel right at home. ∽

The Nonprofits

Poe never made any money from "The Raven," despite the fact that it was hugely popular in his lifetime. Here are artists from other disciplines who suffered similar fates.

Music—Stephen Foster

The Work: "Camptown Races," "Oh! Susanna," and more than 200 other mid-nineteenth-century standards

The Shaft: Foster was the piano-playing Poe, a famous songwriter struggling to make his living at a time when copyright laws were stacked against him. Typically, his songs would earn him a one-time modest fee from sheet-music publishers, who pirated each other's music like it was going out of style. Foster died in poverty at the age of thirty-seven.

Visual Art—Milton Glaser

The Work: "I Love New York" logo, 1977

The Shaft: Glaser designed the red-hearted logo as a pro bono job for the city's Department of Commerce. He received no compensation for the now-ubiquitous image, and he's repeatedly—and graciously—said that he's not bitter about it. However, in 2001, amid the aftermath of the 9/11 attacks, Glaser created a revised version, adding a black mark to represent the fallen Twin Towers. After the *Daily News* published the new design, Glaser received a cease-and-desist order from the company overseeing the copyright to his original logo.

Acting—David Prowse

The Work: Darth Vader, the *Star Wars* trilogy

The Shaft: You know the voice. You know the helmet. But did you know that the actor who actually donned Darth Vader's black suit was a former bodybuilder named David Prowse? Prowse has claimed that, although his contract entitles him to a small percentage of the box-office receipts from two out of the three original *Star Wars* films, he has yet to see dime one. Lucasfilm denies Prowse's claims but doesn't discuss the specifics of its financial arrangements. Either way, the whole thing smells like a disturbance in the force.

Oscar Wilde
(1854–1900)

Abstract: Daring to speak its name
Birth name: Oscar Fingal O'Flahertie Wills Wilde
Birthplace: Dublin, Ireland
Masterwork: *The Importance of Being Earnest*
Demons: Secrecy and exposure

"I, once a lord of language, have no words in which to express my anguish and shame."
—From *De Profundis*, written from prison, 1897

In Victorian England, a culture built on prudery, sex was a taboo subject, and homosexual sex was a crime. The famously flamboyant playwright Oscar Wilde could not enjoy open relationships with any of his male lovers—and indeed married a woman as a sop to cultural pressures. It was part of the double life he was forced to live, a belittling concession made by a natural nonconformist in a repressive society.

Nowhere is the conscripted duality of Oscar Wilde more evident than in *The Importance of Being Earnest*, his brilliantly durable sitcom of manners, which continues to be one of the most evergreen comedies in theater. Oscar was at the height of his fame when he sat down to craft a story with "no real social interest." On a superficial level, he achieved this goal in spades, fleshed out in the feckless über-dandy

Algernon Moncrieff, who finds social obligations so tedious that he fabricates the existence of a sick friend named Bunbury, whom he pretends to be visiting whenever he wants an out. Algy's deceitful habits are matched only by those of his friend Jack Worthing, who has conjured up his own phony alibi, a brother named Ernest, allowing him to make no-questions-asked trips into town.

The story's setup is followed by a farce of the most innocuous, wackiness-ensuing variety, but buried beneath the fluff, and sprinkled with Oscar's rapid-fire one-liners, is the thinly cloaked twinge of closeted repression. Oscar was no stranger to the kind of charades practiced by Algy and Jack, and he soaks his characters in a parallel conceit. For Algy, the practice is so second nature that he verbifies the name of his nonexistent friend. "Bunburying," he tells Jack, saves men from the demands of conventional society—in particular,

> ## "in a culture built on prudery, sex was a taboo subject, and homosexual sex was a crime"

marriage. "A man who marries without knowing Bunbury has a very tedious time of it," he says. Of course, the king of Bunburying was the author himself. Even the word is inside reference to his own Bunburying habits—a combination of Banbury and Sunbury, the towns where Oscar met, and later rendezvoused with, a handsome schoolboy on a train, or so the story goes. *Earnest*, for all its sodden triviality, is simply the expressed frustration of a man forced to live a lie, a man who had the spirited wherewithal to spin that lie into comic brilliance.

The immediate reception of *Earnest* left little doubt that it would be Oscar's masterwork. The play opened on February 14, 1895, to an enthusiastic crowd of high-society Londoners who were aflutter with anticipation over the newest work by the famous farceur. Despite a thunderous response and positive critical reception, however, Oscar would not write another play. The high from the highlight of his career was over before he knew it. It was only four days later that the Marquess of Queensberry, the father of Oscar's much-younger lover, Sir Alfred Douglas, stormed into the Albemarle Club—the bohemian den where Oscar was a member—and left a visitor's card accusing the playwright of "posing" as a sodomite. Against the judgment of his friends, Oscar sued Queensberry for libel, a decision that, in hindsight, seems intentionally risky seeing how easy it was for the Marquess to round up a number of male prostitutes who were willing to testify in his defense. Suddenly, Oscar went from accuser to accused, and three trials later he was convicted of "committing acts of gross indecency with other male persons."

On the plus side, Oscar's conviction exposed the draconian conservatism of antisodomy laws and paved the way for a gay-rights movement that even he could not have imagined.

His legacy, which includes a vast trove of endlessly applicable quotes (see the introduction to this book), is fittingly summed up by a line uttered in his only novel, *The Picture of Dorian Gray*: "Behind every exquisite thing that existed, there was something tragic." Exquisite things aside, one wonders why the playwright did not heed the advice of his friends. Why did he not simply tear up Queensbury's card, ignore the accusation, and call it a night? Perhaps he was simply adamant that he had done nothing wrong. Or maybe he believed he could charm the jury to see things his way. Or maybe, after years of being forced to live a double life, he simply wanted to ensure that future gallivanters would be free to flirt with, pursue, and maybe even marry handsome young strangers on trains. ∽

Egon Schiele
(1890–1918)

Abstract: The naked lurch
Birth name: Egon Schiele
Birthplace: Tulln an der Donau, Austria
Masterwork: Vienna Secession, forty-ninth exhibition
Demons: The elusive female form

"To restrict the artist is a crime. It is to murder germinating life."

—Inscribed on one of his sketches, drawn from prison, 1912

The story could have been ripped from last week's *New York Post*: a thirteen-year-old girl goes missing; police raid the home of the twenty-two-year-old suspect; they make an arrest, and they confiscate more than 100 pornographic images from the premises. But this was not the tale of a deranged handyman or Nigerian senator. It was the story of Egon Schiele, the quietly tortured Austrian Expressionist, whose erotically charged sketches and paintings have helped redraw the ever-nebulous dividing line between art and pornography.

Schiele's distorted, often graphic nude figures may be a century old, but they have not lost their capacity to spellbind, even if they would still make most of us squeamish in the company of our parents. In the rapidly mutating world of pre–World War I Europe, it was precisely Egon's ability to ruffle the complacent masses that led to his arrest, thereby landing him in the middle of a culture war that was dividing the Austro-Hungarian Empire at its core. At the time, Vienna was abuzz with the radical ideas of Sigmund Freud, who used clinical terminology to raise the tolerance level for dirty talk, and yet the conservative towns that surrounded the Austrian capital remained resistant to such open discussions about penis envy and Oedipus complexes. Egon's greatest misstep, in hindsight, might have been when he ditched the cosmopolitan Vienna to set up shop in the insular village of Neulengbach, where the locals did not take kindly to the arrival of the spiky-haired bohemian.

Egon's studio became a favorite hangout for local teenage girls who, bored with small-town life, were perhaps a little too willing to model for the big-city artist. Their easy compli-

> **"the fact that the teenage girl stripped for her older brother sat no better with Egon's family than it would with families today"**

ance fed Egon's intractable obsession with the female body, which first manifested in the artist's psyche at the age of fourteen. His father died of syphilis that year, after a violent struggle for life that taught the young Egon to see the human body as both exaggerated and twisted. He later became enchanted by the form of his younger sister, Gertrude, his first muse and earliest model. Incidentally, the fact that the teenage girl stripped for her older brother sat no better with Egon's family than it would with families today.

But then Egon was not looking to shock sensibilities; he was looking to explore the unknown and forge emotional bonds in the process. By the time he set up his studio in Neulengbach, he had developed a keen ability to connect with his subjects in a way that dissolved the typical artist-model barriers. This was no dirty old man leering at pretty young things. Barely twenty-two, Egon was essentially a curious artist painting his contemporaries. Then again, try telling that to the father of Tatjana von Mossig—the thirteen-year-old girl at the center of Egon's arrest. After running away from home, Tatjana convinced the artist and his lover to take her to Vienna. However, when the girl got cold feet, the three of them returned to Neulengbach to find the townies up in arms. Police raided Egon's studio and confiscated more than 100 paintings and sketches of graphic nude images. The villagers, outraged that their children had been exposed to bold depictions of prostitutes lifting up their skirts and flaunting their vaginas, demanded Egon's head on a plate. In April 1912, Egon was arrested for kidnapping and statutory rape. (Police assumed that he fondled Tatjana as he painted her.) The charges did not stick, however, as Tatjana refused to testify. The artist was eventually convicted of "public immorality," meaning he exposed minors to pornographic images. Egon was sentenced to three days in prison; this was in addition to the twenty-one days he'd already spent in a jail cell waiting for a verdict. The experience changed Egon profoundly, as evidenced by the self-portraits he drew from his cell, in which the twenty-two-year-old appears bearded, beaten, and twice his age.

Of course, Egon's story would hardly be worth mentioning had his preoccupation with the female form spawned the kind of melon-breasted vixens conjured up by today's comic-book fanboys. In contrast, Egon's thoughtful figures, with their forceful lines and muted colors, show a deep sensitivity for his female subjects. And at the same time, one cannot deny the obvious fact that there is a categorically pornographic quality to his work. (The title of his *Reclining Female Nude with Legs Spread* kind of says it all.) Moreover, his use of very young models strikes upon one of the most irreconcilable hypocrisies of contemporary society, which proudly denounces the sexualization of minors but also markets "Juicy" short-shorts to eight-year-old girls.

In a way, however, Egon Schiele was just a victim of bad timing. It wasn't until 1918, years after his conviction, that he landed his first comprehensive exhibition—part of the forty-ninth Vienna Secession, in Zurich. That same year, as bad luck would have it, an influenza pandemic swept the continent, claiming the life of Egon's pregnant wife, Edith. Egon himself succumbed to the virus three days later, on October 31, 1918. He was only twenty-eight.

Parental Advisory

Egon Schiele's arresting nude figures follow in a long tradition of art that pushes society to rethink the definition of obscenity and pornography. Here are a few others from various creative disciplines.

Lolita—Vladimir Nabokov's 1955 story of a middle-aged scholar who runs off with a preteen girl was called "sheer unrestrained pornography" by the editor of the *Sunday Express*. The book was initially rejected by American publishers and banned in France for two years after it first appeared.

A Clockwork Orange—Stanley Kubrick's unflinchingly graphic 1971 drama about London youngsters gone wild was slapped with the dreaded X rating upon its release in the United States, prompting the director to remove thirty seconds of sexually explicit content.

The Perfect Moment—In 1989, this traveling exhibit of works by the photographer Robert Mapplethorpe caused controversy over public funding for the arts. After deeming some of the photos sadomasochistic and homoerotic in nature, the Corcoran Gallery of Art in Washington, D.C., refused to host the exhibit during its national tour. Mapplethorpe passed away that same year due to complications from AIDS.

Frankenchrist—The 1985 album by the California punkers the Dead Kennedys stirred up trouble when a teenage girl purchased the album at a Los Angeles record store. The girl's mother complained to the California Attorney General, and the band was charged with distributing harmful material to minors. The charge stemmed from a graphic H. R. Giger painting known as "Penis Landscape," which was included as a poster. The case ended, poetically enough, with a hung jury.

Egon's final work is a drawing of his wife, finished one day before her death. It is an affecting sketch, in which the dying woman appears placid, collected, and fully clothed. ∾

H. G. Wells
(1866–1946)

Abstract: Mad scientist for hire
Birth name: Herbert George Wells
Birthplace: Bromley, England
Masterwork: *The Time Machine*
Demons: Professional failure and proletariat prejudice

"I dislike the restriction and distortion of knowledge as I dislike nothing else on earth."
—Introduction to *The Fate of Man,* 1939

When H. G. Wells first appeared on the literary scene in the mid-1890s, he was somewhat overshadowed by the French author Jules Verne, who penned such science-themed adventures as *A Journey to the Centre of the Earth.* ("There was a disposition on the part of literary journalists to call me the English Jules Verne," he once griped.) However, considering the public's unwavering taste for high-concept fare over the eleven-plus decades between Wells's debut and whatever big-budget blockbuster J. J. Abrams is producing this week, it's clear that Wells, not Verne, imbued science fiction with the coolness factor that has made it the centerpiece of modern geekological lore. It's hard to imagine how well the genre would have endured without such handy Wellsian gimmicks as time travel, alien invasions, invisibility formulas, and, of course, brooding depictions of future dystopias.

That said, had H. G. Wells's only contribution to science fiction been gimmickry, he might be remembered today as a kind of prop comic, less an English Jules Verne than a literary Carrot Top. His ongoing influence is more the result of one broad stroke of ingenuity that, you might say, put the science in science fiction. A former scientist himself, Wells was the first major writer to approach sci-fi from inside the scientific community—a community he had hoped to take by storm before his own incompetence shut him out. Wells's eventual foray into full-time writing was a reluctant one, an act of desperation brought about by abject failure and a stubborn refusal to accept the socioeconomic limitations imposed by his working-class roots. For all his later accomplishments, he was, at his heart, an angry scientist wannabe.

"Wells was the first major writer to approach sci-fi from inside the scientific community"

Herbert George Wells, or Bertie as his family called him, was born on the lower rung of the late-Victorian middle class. The son of a shopkeeper father and housemaid mother, he grew up in a time of rigid class structures and stifling religious beliefs. His mother believed adamantly that the best possible outcome for Bertie was the life of a tradesman. But menial work depressed Bertie (one early job as a draper's apprentice had him threatening suicide). Despite his mother's mediocre expectations, he never stopped hoping that he might one day eclipse his lot in life through higher education. However, the more he was told to accept his vocational limitations, the more angry and resentful he grew toward the people he believed were narrowing his opportunities. "I thought they had conspired to keep me down," he later wrote. "I hated them as only the young can hate, and it gave me the energy to struggle . . . for knowledge."

For Bertie, knowledge meant devoting his life to science—an endeavor through which he hoped to gain the social legitimacy he so craved. After a few false starts, he won a scholarship to London's Normal School of Science and a chance to study under Thomas Henry Huxley, one of the most renowned names in science. Huxley, known as "Darwin's pit bull," was a fierce defender of the theory of evolution, which was almost as controversial in nineteenth-century England as it is in modern-day Kansas. Bertie saw in Huxley the kind of scientific greatness he wanted for himself.

There was just one problem: H. G. Wells wasn't that great a scientist. He struggled in the classroom, tested poorly on finals, and even botched the occasional lab assignment beyond recognition. Although Wells did manage to graduate with a bachelor's degree in zoology, his visions of scientific greatness dissolved into the ether of trying to make a living. He found work as a science teacher—moonlighting on the side as a journalist to make ends meet—but even that small bit of good fortune came to an end when a bout with tuberculosis forced him to resign. It was a low point from which he almost didn't recover. Having tried in earnest to conquer the one industry that promised to rescue him from a menial fate, H. G. Wells came up an utter failure. It was during this moment of desperation that he conceived of an idea: What if he could apply his knack for writing pop-science journalism to a work of fiction?

As an experiment, Wells chose to develop an idea about a machine that allows people to travel through time. He'd been toying with the notion of time travel since his days at the Normal School, when he'd read a fellow student's paper on a bold new theory of time as a fourth dimension. The idea was a potential high-concept gold mine, and Wells knew it from the beginning. He called it his "peculiar treasure," his trump card, and when he finally played it, it brought him the recognition he always wanted.

The Time Machine was first published in serialized form in the *New Review*, from January through May 1895. Over the next five years, Wells capitalized on the story's success with a slew of sci-fi

Bleak to the Future

H. G. Wells distinguished himself from other science-fiction writers of his era through his unflinching pessimism. Many thinkers of the day saw the new Darwinism as evidence that humanity was destined for progress, but Wells was convinced that humanity, if left unchecked, would just as easily de-evolve into a more primitive state. Here's how those pessimistic predilections shaped his most famous works:

The Invisible Man (1897)

Hook: A megalomaniacal research scientist concocts an opium-based formula that renders him invisible.

Gaping Scientific Inaccuracy: As countless optometrists have pointed out, the invisible man would have been completely blind. If his retina can't absorb light, it can't produce eyesight.

Reigning Pessimistic Message: The quest for power over wisdom will be the downfall of science.

The War of the Worlds (1898)

Hook: Belligerent Martians invade London and wreak havoc.

Lasting Scientific Legacy: Upon its publication, the book sparked the imagination of a sixteen-year-old Robert Goddard, who went on to invent the world's first liquid-powered rocket, ultimately making real spaceflight possible.

Reigning Pessimistic Message: This is what nineteenth-century British imperialism looks like from the other side.

The Time Machine (1895)

Hook: An unnamed time traveler visits a future society in which the human race has diverged into two species—a separation propagated by the divide between the leisure and working classes.

Dazzling Scientific Calculation: The book predates Einstein's concept of "time dilation" by a decade.

Reigning Pessimistic Message: One day you will serve as lunch for the people serving you lunch.

adventures, including *The Island of Doctor Moreau*, *The Invisible Man*, *The War of the Worlds*, and *The First Men in the Moon*. It's no accident that science—the very industry he failed to conquer—is often the target of criticism in these cautionary allegories about the dangers of human progress. Although Wells went on to write well into the twentieth century, he is largely remembered today for those early high-concept adventures that cast the mold for modern science fiction. H. G. Wells may have failed at science, but in the end he was every bit the inventor as the scientists he envied, even if he did break a few test tubes along the way. ～

Dorothy Parker
(1893–1967)

Abstract: Fresh hell hath fury
Birth name: Dorothy Rothschild
Birthplace: Long Branch, New Jersey, USA
Masterwork: The Wisecrack
Demons: Injustice

"It's not the tragedies that kill us. It's the messes. I can't stand messes."
—Interview with *The Paris Review*, 1956

It all started at a press luncheon at the Algonquin Hotel, in midtown Manhattan, where a roomful of writers and journalists showed up largely for the complimentary food. The year was 1919, and the event was set up to welcome home Alexander Woollcott, the famously multichinned *New York Times* drama critic who was returning from the Great War. Among the guests was a twenty-five-year-old editor named Dorothy Parker, who barely spoke a word all evening. The future wisecracking, scotch-swiveling minx who would earn a reputation for bedding every guy in New York was still years away. So were her tumultuous marriages, multiple abortions, and four failed suicide attempts, which included cutting her wrists, drinking shoe polish, and taking large quantities of sedatives and sleeping powder. At this particular luncheon, Dorothy Parker was everything we'd expect Dorothy Parker not to be: shy, unassuming, content to observe. She had never smoked a cigarette, and the taste of booze made her gag. However, these things would soon change as Dorothy unleashed a brilliant knack for wisecrackery that would make her a national sensation.

Dorothy came by her literary career on a whim. In the summer of 1914, when she was not yet twenty, she was working at a dance studio and writing poetry on the side. That was when she caught wind of a little start-up magazine called *Vanity Fair*, launched less than a year earlier by a young publisher named Condé Nast, who himself was a virtual unknown. Figuring she had nothing to lose, Dorothy submitted her poem "Any Porch" to the publication, whose editor, to her surprise, accepted it. Within four years, she would be on the magazine's staff as an editor and theater critic.

"four failed suicide attempts, which included cutting her wrists, drinking shoe polish, and taking large quantities of sedatives and sleeping powder"

As fate would have it, the press luncheon that Dorothy attended that day in 1919 became a daily tradition, beginning as a humble platform for poorly paid *Vanity Fair* editors to vent about Nast—who, as a boss, was apparently no picnic—and growing into the most influential literary group of the Jazz Age. The Algonquin Round Table, as it came to be known, included critics, actors, poets, playwrights, and humorists who would show up each day and engage in sardonic, talk show–like banter that would be reprinted in newspaper columns across the country. It was the term-coining curmudgeon Franklin Pierce Adams, author of the column "The Conning Tower," who most often jotted down Dorothy's daily quips and printed them for posterity. Dorothy's reputation as a maven of sarcasm and sass grew by leaps and bounds. (It's hard to resist someone who, upon hearing about the death of former President Coolidge, remarks, "How can they tell?")

The Round Table was dubbed our national literary Camelot, and Dorothy, our Guinevere. Her popularity as one of the founding members of the group culminated in 1926, with the publication of her poetry collection *Enough Rope*.

From the beginning of her career, Dorothy's poetry revealed apparent scorn for almost everything. "Women: A Hate Song," an early piece published anonymously in *Vanity Fair*, has her ranting about the recipe-hunting, dress-sewing, dinner-making housewives of the 1920s. "I hate women. They get on my nerves," goes the opening sentence. Men were not spared her derision either, as was apparent in the follow-up poem, "Why I Haven't Married," in which she explained that all the men she dated thus far had been idiots.

Enough Rope was a hit with readers and critics. Even the bourgeois fusspots who called it vulgar and frivolous only seemed to increase its coolness factor. Dorothy had made her mark on the literary world in almost every sense, and yet underneath the sarcastic shots she took at life's many disappointments was a deep hatred of the injustices and unfairness that allowed them. As a small child, one of her defining revelations took place after a major blizzard had just dumped several inches of snow on New York City. Dorothy, watching from the warmth of her family's brownstone, could see the day laborers who were tasked with cleaning up the mess. As they shoveled away, Dorothy's rich aunt—"a horrible woman" by Dorothy's account—remarked how nice it was that the snowstorm had provided the men with work. But Dorothy didn't see it that way. "I knew then it was not so nice that men could work for their lives only in desperate weather," she wrote. It was at that moment that she came to see her upper-class family as existing on the wrong side of the line between fairness and unfairness. By 1927, her head spinning from the heights of her popularity, Dorothy was growing "wild with the knowledge of injustice and brutality and misrepresentation." The problem was that she had built her entire career out of taking nothing seriously. She showed no interest in politics, except to take occasional shots at politicians. Women won the hard-earned right to vote in 1920, but in the seven years since, Dorothy herself had not bothered to step into a voting booth. Nevertheless, she began a lifelong commitment to left-wing causes with a trip to Boston, where she was arrested for protesting the executions of Sacco and Vanzetti, the infamous anarchists who were convicted of murder. Unfortunately, what marked a turning point for Dorothy's personal convictions also signaled a decline in her influence. By 1930, the Round Table had dispersed, and her subsequent years as a Hollywood screenwriter and occasional radio commentator never brought her the same level of acclaim.

Dorothy's final years were lonely ones. Returning to New York, she lived with her dog at the Volney residential hotel on the Upper East Side, a neighborhood populated by the recipe-hunting women she once derided in the pages of *Vanity Fair*. The former shrinking violet who gagged at the taste of liquor was now ravished from decades of alcoholism, down to eighty pounds, with failing eyesight.

Turning the Table

In her later years, Dorothy Parker became increasingly critical, not just of the world around her, but also of her own choices. She wrestled with the pestering sensation that her career of quips and one-liners had been a mostly hollow endeavor. Not even the Round Table, the group that catapulted her to fame, was given a free pass. "These were no giants," she said in an interview with the Associated Press. "The Round Table was just a lot of people telling jokes and telling each other how good they were—just a bunch of loudmouths showing off."

In 1965, two years before her death, Dorothy bequeathed her entire estate to Dr. Martin Luther King Jr. It was a final attempt by a dying woman who wanted to enact real change, to combat the injustice she so hated. And it worked. To this day, the NAACP still collects royalties for reprints of Dorothy Parker's work. ～

Chuck Berry
(b. 1926)

Abstract: Breaking the sound barrier
Birth name: Charles Edward Anderson Berry
Birthplace: St. Louis, Missouri, USA
Masterwork: The opening lick of "Johnny B. Goode"
Demons: Separation and segregation

"Prejudice doesn't make me mad. I guess 'pisses me off' is the word."

—Interview with *Esquire* magazine, 2001

Musicologists have long been divided over the invention of rock 'n' roll. Depending on whom you ask, the genre either came about through a disparate mixture of cultural attitudes and musical styles or it came about through Chuck Berry. Either way, it's hard to argue that any other artist has been more responsible for popularizing the steady backbeat, the energetic guitar licks, and the adventurous showmanship that define the form—to say nothing of the youthful marrow that continues to inspire legions of GarageBand soldiers as they set off on the indulgent road to six-string savvy.

Watch old footage of the zoot-suited virtuoso, duckwalking across the stage and singing willful tunes about having no particular place to go, and you will not get the sense that this was a particularly anguished soul. But while Chuck's happy-go-lucky music transcended racial barriers, it did so at a time when his home state of Missouri still had separate drinking fountains. If Berry became a crossover champion of youth culture, it was only through a painful struggle to unify two worlds that did not want to be unified.

For the young Charles Berry, exposure to those two worlds began in Depression-era St. Louis, where soup kitchens and Hooverville settlements were a fact of life for much of the city's African-American population. Charles and his family were spared such poverty. His father, a contractor who often scored lucrative construction jobs in affluent white neighborhoods, kept the family planted firmly in the middle class, putting Charles on a precarious dividing line. As a black boy on the streets of St. Louis, he had no shortage of run-ins with authorities, but then he also enjoyed mucking around the all-white country clubs where his father did construction.

"if Berry became a crossover champion of youth culture, it was only through a painful struggle to unify two worlds that did not want to be unified"

Music in midcentury Missouri, like midcentury Missouri itself, was starkly divided by race. Blacks listened to rhythm and blues; whites, to country and western. There was no middle ground. Charles, meanwhile, found excitement in both genres, and he never understood why the two sounds had to be mutually exclusive—that is, until he tried mixing them in front of a live audience.

By the early 1950s, Chuck Berry and his blues band were playing regular gigs at the Cosmopolitan, a club in East St. Louis, Illinois. The shows were nothing unusual: blues musicians riffing on

Nat King Cole and Muddy Waters songs for largely black audiences. But when Chuck started introducing a few country-and-western twangers into the mix, more and more white listeners began crossing the river from St. Louis to hear "the black hillbilly." Wowing a crossover audience would prove more difficult than simply getting them to show up, however, as the mixed crowds responded unevenly to Chuck's diverse repertoire. White crowds howled enthusiastically to the country-and-western songs, but they couldn't make heads or tails of Chuck's thick urban drawl. The black listeners, meanwhile, nearly laughed Chuck off the stage when he broke out in hillbilly verse. Chuck became increasingly discouraged by what he saw as narrow-mindedness from both sides. Asked later why he insisted on mixing genres, even in the face of so much resistance, he explained, "I was trying to shoot for the entire population instead of just—shall we say, the neighborhood."

Doggedly, he continued to tweak his sound in hopes of striking the right balance. He enunciated his words so good ol' boys could understand his lyrics; he camped up his showmanship during the country numbers so the blues lovers would feel like they were in on a joke at the hillbillies' expense. In the process, he struck upon a formula that would speak not only to both races but also to the emerging teenage culture as a whole.

Teenagers, as a marketing demographic, were still a new phenomenon in 1955. Postwar prosperity was producing a generation of idle youngsters with extra pocket cash to slurp down malts, go to drive-in movies, and, of course, buy records. It was precisely this denim-clad, poodle-skirted demographic that Chuck had in mind when, in May of that year, he recorded his first single for the independent label Chess Records. "Maybellene," a spunky, guitar-fueled rendition of the old hillbilly standard "Ida Red," became a runaway hit with teenagers of all stripes. It was one of the first records to reach the *Billboard* charts for blues, country, and pop music.

It should come as no surprise that not everyone was ready to embrace a genre that encouraged interracial mingling. For every bobbysoxer bouncing up and down at one of Chuck's shows, there was a sign-wielding parent yawping about the obscene devil's music. At one gig in Jacksonville, Florida, Chuck recalled ropes being tied across the center of the aisle to keep the races apart. The ropes were torn down by the show's end, with the entire audience dancing together. Chuck Berry, at the ripe old age of twenty-nine, was leading the charge for a new generation of colorblind audiences. His subsequent hits remain standards of late-fifties enthusiasm: "Roll Over Beethoven," a youthful ode to the triumph of low culture over high; "Rock and Roll Music," a celebration of the genre itself; "Johnny B. Goode," a semiautobiographical ditty about a poor country boy who finds his salvation in music.

Unfortunately, the decade that Chuck helped define would, for him, end on a sour note. In December 1959, he was arrested for transporting a minor across state lines. After two trials and two appeals, he ultimately served an eighteen-month prison sentence, from February 1962 to October 1963. Upon his release, he resumed his music career only to discover that the genre he pioneered was already changing. The rockabilly-inspired grease balls of just a few years ago were being drowned out by the harmonies of moppy-headed Brits. By the time the Beatles played Sullivan the following year, Chuck Berry seemed

My Payola

Chuck Berry's breakthrough hit, "Maybellene," never would have made it on the air had it not been for a shady little side deal between Chess Records and the popular deejay Alan Freed, who is credited with coining the term "rock 'n' roll." Chess agreed to give Freed a cocomposer credit on the song in exchange for heavy airplay. The credit entitled Freed to a cut of the royalties—a nice little incentive for stepping up "Maybellene" in the rotation. And that's just what he did, playing the song every two hours on his 1010 WINS radio show in New York City. A few years later, when authorities started cracking down on payola scandals, Freed was busted and thrown off the air.

like a Ford Model T in a Cadillac showroom. But even though the legacy police have been perhaps a little too kind to those British invaders of the sixties, at least the musicians themselves knew when to credit their roots. In fact, it was John Lennon who said it best: "If you tried to give rock 'n' roll another name, you might call it 'Chuck Berry.'" ∿

6

Precarious Partnerships

The Fine Line Between Harmony and Friction

Given the propensity of tortured artists to clash with one another, it's easy to imagine what happens when the careers of two artists become immutably tied together. Such ventures often result in the kind of friction that, despite damaging relationships, becomes the very thing that fuels the art.

While collaboration is as old as art itself, creative partnerships are a relatively new concept. In the 1890s, the vaudeville slapstickers Weber and Fields became two of the first performers to market themselves successfully as a comic duo. Such duos emerged as one of the bedrock formulas of twentieth-century comedy. Laurel and Hardy, Burns and Allen, Abbott and Costello—each of these teams achieved a level of success that eclipsed the performers within them. Among these interminably tied comic couplings, one Hollywood duo stands out as an exception to the paragons of longevity. Dean Martin and Jerry Lewis, who built their careers as a comedy team in nightclubs, in movies, and on radio and television, managed to effectively break away from each other, concluding a relatively short ten-year run after vicious animosity tore them apart. In 1956, after five years at Paramount Pictures, Dean had grown tired of playing the sterile straight man to Jerry's wacky, but far more interesting, characters. He was

Dean Martin and Jerry Lewis

being outshined by Jerry's bucktoothed buffoonery, and he knew it. However, when *LOOK* magazine ran a cover story on Martin and Lewis—but cropped Dean out of the picture—Dean realized he'd had enough. After telling Jerry, "To me, you're nothing but a fucking dollar sign,"

Dean ended the partnership. It was one of the most famously contentious breakups in showbiz history, and it would be another thirty-three years before the two reunited, at the Bally's Hotel and Casino in Las Vegas, for one final performance.

In more recent decades, the songwriting collaboration between John Lennon and Paul McCartney has stood as one of the defining examples of creative friction and its potential to produce harmonious results. With distinctly different styles, the two songwriters often did not see eye-to-eye on the direction of a song. And yet both their styles proved to be correct. It wasn't John's raw edge or Paul's melodic sensibilities that made the Beatles more than the sum of their disjointed parts. It was the combination of the two.

As we'll see with the following case studies, Lennon-McCartney–type friction is a common element in creative partnerships, which, like marriages, exist for better or worse.

Gilbert and Sullivan

(1836–1911/1842–1900)

Abstract: The operatic odd couple
Birth names: William Schwenck Gilbert/Arthur Seymour Sullivan
Birthplace: London, England
Co-venture: The Savoy Operas
Demons: Fantasy and reality

"You say that in serious opera you must, more or less, sacrifice yourself. I say that this is just what I have been doing in all our joint pieces."
—**Sullivan in a letter to Gilbert, 1889**

Musical theater, like sex, will always suffer under the weight of over-analysis. How much would we enjoy the genre if we were to stop and think about the sheer absurdity of finger-snapping gang members in New York City, or singing Mormons in northern Uganda, or twirling hippies at a war protest? (Okay, the hippie one is believable.) The fact is, the success of musical theater is rooted in our ability to accept the ridiculous, and our familiarity with that ridiculousness is rooted in the contemptuous relationship between W. S. Gilbert and Arthur Sullivan, whose anomalous mixture of logic and whimsy helped lay the groundwork for the conventions of the format.

Back in the 1850s, British theater was about as well respected as British cuisine. Although Blighty audiences did have a few sophisticated options—overproduced Shakespeare tragedies, for instance—most of what took place on West End stages was the lower ends of the low brow. There were racy burlesques, raunchy farces, and poorly translated French operettas galore, but there was not a whole lot of middle ground, to say nothing of family-friendly fare. W. S. Gilbert, a former barrister who got his start writing illustrated comic poems for humor magazines, thought stage comedy should aim higher. His methodical mind, pounded into submission by years of legal training, did not take kindly to the kind of anarchistic, pie-in-the-face-style wackiness that ruled the day. Comic characters, he thought, should not be aware of their own absurdity, but rather they should be bound by the absurd as if it were completely logical. His views on naturalistic theater were particularly progressive considering that, at

"the success of musical theater is rooted in our ability to accept the ridiculous"

the time, Ibsen had yet to establish himself and G. B. Shaw was still a schoolboy. When he began working on comic operas at John Hollingshead's Gaiety Theatre, Gilbert quickly established himself as one of the top librettists in the country. The problem was that his middlebrow aims were too highbrow. He was too intellectual for his own good.

Fortunately, fate intervened. When Hollingshead needed an operatic extravaganza for the Christmas season of 1871, he teamed up Gilbert with the young songsmith Arthur Sullivan, a rising star among orchestral composers. That first collaboration, *Thespis*, would be billed as Sullivan and Gilbert, a credit order that would soon switch. Sullivan may have been the bigger name, but Gilbert was the bigger personality. A tall, perpetually scowling control freak, he was already thirty-five years old when he met the twenty-nine-year-old Sullivan, who, for the most part, avoided conflict. If all signs pointed to the fact that the duo would be better off without each other, Gilbert and Sullivan were nevertheless pulled together by a shared hope: They both wanted to use comic opera as a stepping stone to more serious work. Sullivan had dreams of writing a weighty spectacle in the vein of Verdi or Wagner. Gilbert looked forward to the day when he would be considered a master dramatist. Still, with commercial concerns to consider, they were willing to collaborate—for the time being—on fluffy material that each felt was beneath his potential.

What neither expected, however, was to hit upon a theatrical formula that would make them international sensations, promulgated by the runaway success of their fourth musical collaboration, *H.M.S. Pinafore*, a boy-meets-girl satire of the British Navy under Queen Victoria. Despite *The Daily Telegraph*'s assessment that the play was "a frothy production destined soon to subside into nothingness," *Pinafore* was a smash. Within six months, it made its way stateside, premiering in Boston and then spreading to cities across the country. Gilbert and Sullivan staged their first authorized production in November 1879, but by then some 150 pirated productions had already been mounted. It was so popular that some cities had multiple productions, by multiple theater companies, running in tandem. The widespread unauthorized productions of the operetta inspired the team's next collaboration, *The Pirates of Penzance*.

Pirates was another monster hit for Gilbert and Sullivan, but behind the scenes, theater's newest dynamic duo were two bickering opponents who watched in frustration as their names became inexorably intertwined. The now-famous Savoy Theatre was built around their successful partnership, and before long, hundreds of jobs depended on the continued solvency of the Gilbert and Sullivan brand. And yet the two of them could not even agree on subject matter. Sullivan, a monocle-wearing fop, enjoyed the finer things in life, and he resented Gilbert's middlebrow story lines, which essentially centered on poking fun at the upper classes. The duo had such trouble getting along that they often needed third-party mediation to work out their differences. It's all one can do to imagine that they wrote their famous "What never? Well, hardly ever" bit while ripping out each other's mutton chops.

For the most part, the partnership was kept functional by Gilbert's dominating personality, which is to say that Gilbert usually got his way. It was the kind of working relationship that hinged upon one man's ability to take another man's crap. In later years, though, Sullivan became more determined to throw off the yoke and pursue his dream of writing a serious opera.

"I have lost the liking for writing comic opera," he wrote to Gilbert. What he really lost was the liking for being subservient to his partner, who, despite his obtuseness, understood that his words needed Sullivan's music. In a rare display of humility, Gilbert attempted to appease Sullivan, assuring him that the two could collaborate "as master and master—not master and servant." But in 1894, when Gilbert readied his latest story, *His Excellency,* Sullivan refused to score it after the two men disagreed over casting. The partnership, after twenty-five years and fourteen comic operas, came to an end. *His Excellency*, for what it's worth, later opened to mixed reviews. Critics loved Gilbert's libretto but hated F. Osmond Carr's score.

In 1904, four years after Arthur Sullivan passed away, the *London Times* wrote an article that criticized the deteriorating quality of the operas being produced at the Savoy Theatre. W. S. Gilbert, now in his mid-sixties, quickly fired off a letter to the editor, stating what he believed to be the true cause of the decline. "Savoy Opera was snuffed out by the deplorable death of my distinguished collaborator, Sir Arthur Sullivan," he wrote. "When that event occurred, I saw no one with whom I felt that I could work with satisfaction and success." Perhaps the famously stubborn librettist was just being diplomatic, or maybe he had finally accepted that his legacy would be forever tied to that of his late associate. Either way, the blustery partnership of Gilbert and Sullivan lives on in the belting and gamboling of modern musical theater. For escapists who still gush in excitement over the latest Broadway extravaganza, musical theater offers an irresistible marriage of logic and absurdity. For the duo who started it all, however, it was just a marriage of convenience. ∿

Lucille Ball and Desi Arnaz
(1911–1989/1917–1986)

Abstract: The out-of-touch-with-reality show
Birth names: Lucille Désirée Ball/ Desiderio Alberto Arnaz y de Acha III
Birthplaces: Jamestown, New York, USA/Santiago de Cuba, Cuba
Co-venture: *I Love Lucy*
Demons: Marriage and infidelity

"Friends gave our marriage six months; me, I gave it a week."
—**Lucille Ball, from her autobiography, 1996**

Sometimes the chocolates tumble down the conveyor belt faster than we can wrap them. That famous scene in which Lucy Ricardo and Ethel Mertz, decked out in baker hats, botch their first day of work in a candy factory stands as the perfect metaphor for those times when we have simply bitten off more than we can chew. It's also an apt analogy for the mutually abusive relationship between Lucille Ball and Desi Arnaz, the power couple behind Desilu Studios and the landmark sitcom *I Love Lucy*. For two dominating personalities, the task of trying to tame each other ultimately became more than they could handle.

Lucille Ball never envisioned that she would one day become America's screwball sweetheart. Back in the 1930s, the former Hattie Carnegie fashion model aspired to Hollywood glamour under the old studio system, sporting platinum-blonde locks as a would-be Harlow for RKO Pictures. It was on the set of the 1940 film *Dance, Girl, Dance* that she met Desi Arnaz, a Cuban-born bandleader and Broadway actor who had just arrived in Hollywood.

On their first date, Lucille and Desi instantly connected over parallel stories of family tragedy. Desi told Lucille about how his father was once the mayor of Santiago, in Cuba. After the Cuban revolution of 1933, the government collapsed, and the elder Arnaz went into exile in the United States. Desi followed when he was seventeen, only to find his father living in a rat-infested warehouse. As it happened, Lucille experienced an eerily similar incident in her past. When she was fif-

> **"both were angry at the unjust world that let it happen, and both were determined to vindicate their family names through a career in Hollywood"**

teen, her grandfather Fred, who raised her, was supervising a target-shooting game at Lucille's childhood home near Jamestown, New York. A neighborhood boy was accidentally shot and paralyzed on the property, and Fred was sued for negligence by the boy's family. The Balls were wiped out. If ever there were a bittersweet first-date bonding moment, it was this one.

Lucille and Desi were kindred victims, refugees of familial ruin who had seen their father figures reduced to nothing through external circumstances. Both were angry at the unjust world that let it happen, and both were determined to vindicate their family names through a career in Hollywood.

But it was more than just bitterness that ignited the couple's passions. A spark-inducing physical attraction was apparent from the beginning, when Lucille fell in love with Desi "wham, bang!" as she put it. Lucille and Desi, in their first few months together, were joined at the hip and everywhere else, making out at nightclubs and generally pushing the bounds of acceptable PDA. Yes, they were *that* couple.

And when that couple eloped in 1940, it was a personal turning point for Lucille. Driven and ambitious, the fiery ginger had spent her youth courting powerful, usually much older men who could help her career. Desi was six years her junior and lower on the showbiz ladder—not her usual type to say the least. But he was such a commanding and charismatic force that Lucille resolved, for the first time in her life, to play second fiddle. Their plan was simple: Desi was going to take over Hollywood, and Lucille would help.

Unfortunately, life had other plans for the couple. By the end of the 1940s, Lucille was still the breadwinner, with a lucrative career as a B-movie queen. She had also begun to find her comedic chops, working as a voice actress on the CBS radio program *My Favorite Husband*. Desi, meanwhile, continued to struggle as a part-time nightclub performer and full-time hedonist. He drank heavily, gambled compulsively, and philandered like a postapocalyptic survivor trying to repopulate the species. Desi hated being second best. He had come to Hollywood to conquer but found himself in the shadow of a more successful wife. As for the love-blinded Lucille, she convinced herself that Desi's transgressions were not a symptom of character flaws but a consequence of his profession. His gigs as a bandleader kept him on the road for months at a time, gallivanting with, of all people, musicians. If she could just keep the guy at home, she knew he would behave himself.

By the beginning of the 1950s, the studio system that had been Lucille's primary source of revenue was under threat. Fewer

Americans were going to the theater, and the movie industry was growing increasingly anxious over its new competition: television. So when CBS executives approached Lucille with an offer to star in a TV version of *My Favorite Husband*, the actress was understandably hesitant. Television was the enemy, after all, and if the show failed, her movie career might not recover. That was when it struck her that she could parlay the series into an opportunity to domesticate her promiscuous consort. Of course, she knew executives would be reluctant to cast Desi as her TV husband—his broken English did not exactly scream all-American man—but Lucille stood her ground. She was tired of watching her marriage decay at the seams, and her only hope was to merge Desi's professional world with hers. She told producers flat out: Cast Desi or no deal.

After the requisite hemming and hawing, CBS agreed, and the show was retooled as *I Love Lucy*, a comedy about the all-American couple with a Latin twist. The Ricardos, however, were less a fictionalized version of Lucille and Desi than an act of Bizzaro World wish fulfillment. In the show, Ricky was the successful showman while his wife, Lucy, was the antic-prone screwball with dreams of breaking into the business. This was Lucille and Desi as they had always wanted to be.

Of course, if you've seen one wacky couple, you've seen them all, and the real innovation of *I Love Lucy* was not its premise but its execution. Lucille and Desi used their combined experience on radio, Broadway, and in movies to create a completely novel format for a medium that was still trying to figure out its potential. In the days before video, TV was largely a point-and-shoot business. Episodes were broadcast live, one time, and never seen again. But Desi had the idea to shoot *Lucy* on 35 mm film, in sequence, from multiple angles—staging the show like a play, in front of a live audience, and broadcasting it later. CBS balked at the idea. Film was expensive, and what would the network have to gain from it? It was only after Lucy and Desi agreed to a take a reduced salary that the network gave in. For evidence of just how tremendously Desi's gamble paid off, watch old footage of *I Love Lucy* in comparison to other fuzzy-pictured specimens of early television. *Lucy* is crisp, dynamic, and not all that different from sitcoms today. Moreover, its film-based genesis gave it a shelf life that lasted far beyond its original airdate, making Lucy and Desi pioneers of a concept that proved endlessly lucrative—the rerun.

I Love Lucy, with its three-camera, live-audience setup, turned sitcoms into a television mainstay. Admittedly, viewing habits have changed since Lucy and Ethel got bombarded at that chocolate factory. Audiences today might be more likely to watch a reality show set in the high-stakes world of candy manufacturing. But listen carefully and you will still hear the familiar sound of laugh tracks under the obnoxious din of such unscripted fare. Sitcoms are here to stay, even if the real-life relationship between Lucille and Desi was not so durable. In the end, the Ricardos were a fantasy, created by two dominant personalities who wanted, more than anything, to be the Ricardos. When they finally went off the air, in 1957, the fantasy ended. Lucille and Desi divorced less than three years later. ∽

Johnny and Joey Ramone
(1948–2004/1951–2001)

Abstract: Gabba gabba hate
Birth names: John William Cummings/Jeffry Ross Hyman
Birthplace: Queens, New York, USA
Co-venture: The Ramones
Demons: Order and chaos

"We didn't agree on anything. Joey was a thorn in my side."

—Johnny Ramone in his final interview, *Spin* magazine, 2004

In the spring of 1974, Richard Nixon's presidency wasn't the only thing that needed saving. Rock music was in some serious trouble as well. The genre was pushing twenty, and the peppy simplicity championed by early practitioners such as Chuck Berry and Buddy Holly had given way to self-indulgent excess. Guitar solos could last into the night. Concept albums were overproduced to the point of psychedelic futility. Even Don McLean lamented Holly's death as the end of a simpler era, but then he didn't seem to notice that "American Pie" was almost nine minutes long. Something had to be done.

    Enter John Cummings, a cranky, aggressive, bowl-haired delinquent from the Forest Hills section of Queens. Born in 1948, John was part of the first generation to grow up with rock 'n' roll, and he had come to believe that the meandering jams of Deep Purple and the Grateful Dead had strayed too far from the straightforward sound he loved as a child. John had heard enough. At the age of twenty-five, he "stopped listening to everything," bought a $50 guitar, and vowed to start his own band, one that would adopt the stripped-down style of the 1950s. He couldn't play very well, but he had the laser-sharp focus of a pit bull on ginkgo, and he could down-stroke like nobody's business. He knew three chords, and that was enough.

But something was missing from John's new musical venture. It had plenty of heart, but not much soul. That's where a neighborhood friend named Jeffry Hyman, a.k.a. Joey, came in. Joey and John inhabited opposite ends of the crazy meter. Whereas John could stare into the barrel of a gun without flinching, Joey saw the world as an intensely frightening place. Shortly after birth, he had a baseball-sized growth removed from his spine—the result of a phantom twin—and the crescent-shaped scar it left on his back stood as a terrifying reminder that death could strike at any time. His lanky, 6'6" frame marked him as the very embodiment of gracelessness and frailty.

"his behavior was seen as nothing more than a harmless annoyance until the night he pulled a knife on his mother in an unprovoked fit of paranoia"

The teenager Joey's home life was a sideshow of bizarre habits. When he was not twiddling his hair or tapping his fingers, he was opening and closing doors or switching lights on and off until the wee hours of the morning. His behavior was seen as nothing more than a harmless annoyance until the night he pulled a knife on his mother in an unprovoked fit of paranoia, resulting in a trip to the psychiatric wing of St. Vincent's Hospital for evaluation. The verdict? Paranoid schizophrenia and obsessive-compulsive disorder. There was no getting around it. Joey was certifiable, with the papers to prove it, but his introversion and wandering mind equipped him with a childlike sensibility. In short, he was a natural dreamer who understood the abstract sensitivity that John's band was missing. As luck would have it, the kid could also croon like a fuzzy-voiced Bobby Darin.

In August 1974, the Ramones played their first gig with Joey on vocals. It was at a tiny club on the Bowery, a hole in the wall called CBGB, which had opened a few months earlier as a platform for country, bluegrass, and blues. The crude combo from Queens fell into none of those categories. In fact, there was no genre to describe them at all.

The Ramones were a retro retread of fifties rock 'n' roll, bolstered by the wattage of seventies amps, turbocharged with John's natural aggression, and finessed with Joey's ear for bubblegum melodies.

Outwardly, the Ramones presented a united front, donning identical leather jackets, long hair, and stone-faced expressions. Internally, however, they were four squabbling spouses whose domestic strife was exacerbated by the fact that the militant John could not get the unstable Joey to bend to his dictates. From the beginning of their collaborative partnership, Joey and John felt an almost constant animosity toward each other. What neither of them had counted on, however, was getting caught up in a burgeoning underground scene whose very ethos was built around the kind of antipathetic feelings they harbored toward each other. Disaffected young music fans, fed up with corporate-sanctioned rock, flocked to CBGB in search of a more aggressive sound. They found it in the ever-infighting Ramones, who quickly developed a devoted following along with fellow noise-makers such as Patti Smith, Talking Heads, and Blondie. In January 1976, the local music fanzine *Punk* published its first issue, and suddenly the scene had a name. For Joey and John, there was no going back.

Mutual dislike aside, the final nail in the coffin of Joey and John's relationship was yet to come. In 1978, Joey started dating Linda Danielle, a high-maintenance lovely who preferred expensive clothes and jewelry to ripped jeans and Chuck Taylors. For a while, it looked as though Linda could be the stabilizing presence that Joey had long needed, but the couple was ill matched, and Linda knew it. When she dumped him, Joey was devastated; when she started dating Johnny, he was permanently wounded. In Johnny's defense, he and Linda eventually got married and stayed together until his death, but the Ramones were never the same. Joey and Johnny, once mere antagonists, became bitter enemies. And yet, as if locked in a game of chicken, neither member would quit the band. What choice did they have? It was stay in the Ramones, or get real jobs.

After that incident, Joey and Johnny's best collaborating days were behind them, and yet they had already planted the seeds that would radically, if indirectly, change the face of rock music. After playing a few gigs in London, in 1976, the Ramones caught the attention of a handful of disaffected young musicians. Within a year, British punk rock exploded, fronted by the Sex Pistols, the Clash, and other spiky-haired sneersters. The punk sound ricocheted back to the United States, seeping its way into underground clubs, from D.C. to San Francisco. A host of 1980s genres followed: new wave, heavy metal, hardcore, ska. But the Ramones' influence didn't end there. In the 1990s, the group's blend of melodic aggression was slowed down, repackaged as grunge, and taken into the mainstream by groups like Nirvana and Pearl Jam. Throughout, the Ramones continued to tour—with Joey and Johnny barely speaking—until finally breaking up in 1996. By then, the punk mindset had become an institution within music circles, a raw and resistant philosophy that would not see its official demise until 2010, when Green Day's *American Idiot* premiered on Broadway. Punk rock was fashioned out of a conflict between two polar opposites: a restless fighter and a hopeless dreamer. As for the band that started it all, despite having propelled the direction of rock music for the better part of thirty years, the Ramones never had a single chart-topping hit. ∼

Ike and Tina Turner
(1931–2007/b. 1939)

Abstract: Who needs a heart?
Birth names: Ike Wister Turner/ Anna Mae Bullock
Birthplaces: Clarksdale, Mississippi/Nutbush, Tennessee, USA
Co-venture: The Ike and Tina Turner Revue
Demons: Power and submission

"I didn't know how to get out of the whole situation. There were many times when I picked up the gun when he was sleeping."
—Interview with Oprah Winfrey, 2005

In 1956, Ike Turner was closer to music stardom than most musicians will ever get. The front man for a spunky blues band called Kings of Rhythm, he had achieved local-celebrity status around the bustling environs of greater St. Louis, where he drew eager crowds and played to small but packed houses. Much to his own frustration, however, Ike seemed to have hit a celebrity ceiling. The national prominence he hopelessly sought continued to elude him, and despite having recorded the 1951 chart-topper "Rocket 88," he was living in constant fear that he would one day vanish in a flicker of one-hit-wonder oblivion. For the wayward aspirant who wanted desperately to be a star, Ike Turner was missing one key ingredient: star quality.

But Ike's fate would change with the arrival of Anna Mae Bullock, a teenage transplant from the rustic hills of western Tennessee who had taken to girls' nights out in East St. Louis, where Ike was headlining at Club Manhattan. At first glance, Anna Mae found the gold-chain-wearing slickster repulsive. ("His teeth seemed all wrong, and his hairstyle, too," she balked.) But when he played his guitar, the young girl lapsed into a trance. It wasn't a sexual attraction, mind you. Rather it was girlish awe for a dedicated showman who commanded both his instrument and the crowd. In any case, Ike's flat-bodied presence was enough to rope her in. One night, in between sets, Anna Mae grabbed the microphone, showed off her raspy pipes to the tune of B. B. King's "You Know I Love You," and roped Ike right back.

Blown away by her singing, Ike saw in the young girl the true star potential that he secretly knew he lacked. To top it off, Ike was a leg man, and Anna Mae had a set that seemed to go on forever.

Within a year, Anna Mae and her legs were fronting Ike's group. Ike dressed her up in sequins, rechristened her Tina—a name she despised—and soon the duo was touring the country as the Ike and Tina Turner Revue. With Anna Mae's peppery vocals and energetic moves on display, the group rose to fame as one of the most adventurous rhythm-and-blues acts in the country, starting with their 1960 hit, "A Fool in Love." Ike and Tina had extraordinary longevity, peaking between 1964 and 1974, and culminating with their biggest hit, the Grammy-winning "Proud Mary," in 1971. The song is a ceremonious epic, fleshed out by Anna Mae's sultry opening, which builds at a leisurely pace only to explode with the orchestral blast of Ike's rhythmic authority. And yet, underlying Ike and Tina's dynamic stage chemistry—an irresistible blend of soul and sass—lived a cruel tension, fueled by Ike's physical and mental abuse. Anna Mae, the wild woman of soul, who would flood the stage, screeching and flailing like a trapped animal, was secretly channeling the torment of emotional imprisonment.

Ike's power-wielding personality was not initially apparent to the naive Anna Mae. At first they were more like brother and sister;

however, those boundaries quickly dissolved one night on the road, when Ike got frisky and Anna Mae was too intimidated to resist his pushy advances. "I had never thought of having sex with him," she later recalled. "I thought, 'God, this is horrible.'" That dubious consummation set into motion a pattern of power and control that would last for sixteen years, growing incrementally more brutal and continuing through marriage, a child, and the group's eventual decline. During that time, Ike allegedly beat Anna Mae with anything that wasn't nailed down, including shoes, telephones, wire hangers, and his bare knuckles. He broke her ribs, arm, and jaw, and once even threw hot coffee in her face. When she protested, he questioned her loyalty. And when she tried to leave him, he would track her down. In a veritable Dark Ages for abused spouses—predating the widespread accessibility of battered women's shelters—Anna Mae was cornered, helpless under the dominating force of an incurable showman who would not give up his golden goose.

"he broke her ribs, arm, and jaw, and once even threw hot coffee in her face"

Ike, for his part, always maintained that allegations of his abuse were overblown. (In his autobiography, he admits to slapping and punching Tina but seems to deny that such behavior constitutes "beating.") Nevertheless, his years of beating Anna Mae were ultimately undone by his beating himself. As the mid-seventies rolled on, and he drowned himself in a glut of cocaine, prescription pills, and other women, Anna Mae turned to Buddhism and got in touch with her inner strength. She continued, meanwhile, to act as the face of Ike and Tina, often making solo TV appearances while Ike was too drugged to join her.

In 1976, Ike and Anna Mae had one final physical confrontation, on the road in Dallas. Ike backhanded her in a limousine, and Anna Mae thought, "Today I'm fighting back." Later that day, when her husband predictably passed out in their hotel room, Anna Mae seized the opportunity and fled the scene, thirty-six cents and a gas card to her name. The couple's divorce was finalized some two years later, with Anna Mae agreeing to give Ike all the group's monetary assets. It was a concession she made only on the condition that she be allowed the continued use of her stage name, Tina Turner, a star persona created for her by a wannabe star who kept her in emotional bondage. ∼

Portrait of a Vicious Cycle

The violent details of Ike Turner's childhood practically scream "future abuser." When he was eight years old, he witnessed his father beaten to near death by a white mob. Ike's father was denied admission into a whites-only hospital and subsequently lived as an invalid in a tent in the family's backyard, finally succumbing to his injuries three years later. Ike later tried to bludgeon his new stepfather to death after the man whipped him with barbed wire. By the age of eighteen, Ike was sporting two gunshot wounds and had earned the nickname Pistol Whippin' Turner.

Werner Herzog and Klaus Kinski

(b. 1942/1926–1991)

Abstract: The frenemy within
Birth names: Werner Herzog Stipetić/Klaus Günter Karl Nakszynski
Birthplaces: Munich, Germany/ Sopot, Danzig (now Poland)
Co-venture: New German Cinema
Demons: Each other

"Every grey hair on my head I call Kinski."
—From *Herzog on Herzog*, 2003

Modern cinema is built around successful director/actor partnerships —Scorsese and De Niro; Burton and Depp; Apatow and goofy guys with curly hair; the list goes on. Of course, the success of such partnerships hinges on an often-delicate balancing act between actors who know how to take direction and directors who know how to give it. And yet some of the most influential movements in cinema history came about through the complete dissolution of the kind of egg-shell-walking niceties that most of us expect from a workplace. Case in point: the feud-filled relationship between Werner Herzog and Klaus Kinski. Over the strained course of their fifteen-year, five-film collaboration, this combustible pair of love-hate antagonists discovered they had two choices: They could capture the volatility between them on screen, or they could kill each other. They managed the former only by coming dangerously close to the latter.

Long before Werner Herzog rose to art-house glory as one of the quintessential auteurs of the New German Cinema, he knew he was destined to make movies. A sternly intelligent and obsessive youth, he began sending scripts to German film producers when he was still in his early teens. He financed his first film, a nine-minute short called *Herakles*, while working as a welder in a steel factory in 1961. The next year, he joined twenty-five other filmmakers in signing the *Oberhausen Manifesto*, a bold call to arms by disillusioned young directors who vowed to end the creative stagnation of Germany's movie industry.

To Werner, the vow was more than lip service; it was the solemn mission of an impulsive director who preferred to shoot first and ask questions later—a man who so detested wasteful introspection that he claimed not to know the color of his own eyes. But to realize such a dense singular vision, the kind only a manifesto could communicate, Herzog would need a leading man whose denseness matched his own. The young director found his equal in Klaus Kinski, a self-taught actor who had such a difficult time working with others that he mostly made do as a monologist.

Werner first met the unpredictable actor when the two were both living at a Munich boarding house, where Kinski would terrorize the other residents by trashing assorted pieces of furniture. Those early days, however unsettling to the teenage Werner, encumbered the director with indelible memories of a raving madman who foamed at the mouth and threw tantrums at the drop of a hat. In 1971, when it came time to cast the lead in his fourth film, *Aguirre, the Wrath of God,* Werner had only one choice in mind to play the title character, a delusional conquistador who leads his men on a quest to find the fabled city of gold, El Dorado.

During the five-week shoot on location in the Peruvian rainforest, Kinski lived up to his reputation, with a surplus of lunacy to spare. He lambasted crewmembers, frightened the locals, and threw tantrums over everything from Herzog's directing style to the wet Peruvian weather. In one instance, he became annoyed by the carryings on of some of the crew and wound up shooting off an extra's finger-tip with a rifle. Werner, in turn, threw Klaus's tempestuous behavior right back in his face. When he wasn't threatening his leading man with gunfire, he was deliberately egging him on in whatever manner necessary to aid the project, a means of "domesticating the beast," as he put it. If Werner needed a quieter performance from the actor, he would purposely push Klaus's buttons, wait for him to explode, and capture his posttantrum exhaustion for the scene.

Whatever he did worked. When it was released in 1972, *Aguirre, the Wrath of God* emerged as a career-defining cult hit, securing Werner's place as an early pioneer of the coming independent film movement. (It may also be one of the most successful movies ever shot

"at the climax of their association, they were simultaneously plotting to kill each other"

with a stolen camera.) Meanwhile, Werner and Klaus's relationship remained gravely intractable throughout their fifteen-year collaboration. At the climax of their association, they were simultaneously plotting to kill each other, with Herzog at one point attempting to firebomb Kinski's house. And yet, like alchemic serendipity, their combustible interactions always managed to serve the greater good of Herzog's films.

For all their frenzied exchanges, Werner and Klaus shared the same deep sense of self-sacrifice, willing to put themselves in personal jeopardy for the sake of the project at hand. When Klaus was filming a scene for 1979's *Woyzeck*—in which his character gets kicked to the ground by a drill major—the actor was not satisfied with his scene partner's simulated assault. "He's not doing it right," Klaus insisted to Werner. "He has to *really* kick me." The other actor reluctantly obliged, kicking Klaus so hard into the cobblestone street that his face began to puff up, and Werner wasted no time capturing the damage. (Watch the film's opening-credit sequence, in which half of Klaus's face looks like a Pillsbury muffin.)

Werner and Klaus's relationship finally became irreconcilable on the set of the 1987 film *Cobra Verde*, when Klaus's outbursts had gotten so out of hand that neither Werner nor his crew could bear them. *Cobra* was the duo's final collaboration before Klaus's fatal heart attack in 1991. Eight years later, Werner released a documentary about his relationship with the actor. Aptly titled *My Best Fiend*, the film presents with surprising warmth a man who had been at once the filmmaker's best friend and greatest foe—a personal demon personified. "We had a mutual respect for each other," Werner admitted, "even as we planned each other's murders."

That mutual respect, though buried beneath the raving-mad mannerisms of two thickheaded souls, was nevertheless evident from both parties. Publicly, Kinski claimed to despise the films he made with Werner. (In his autobiography, he castigated the filmmaker as a no-talent megalomaniac.) And yet he knew, deep down, that only Werner could do his performances justice. Kinski often complained about the scant salaries he made on low-budget films. He had no compunction about turning down a role if the price wasn't right, and one time he even shunned an offer from Fellini, whom he dismissed as low-paying "vermin." But for Werner Herzog's micro-budget efforts, he always made an exception. The pay may not have been great, but the fights were a nice perk. ∾

7

Substance
over Style

Welcome to Oz (Where Even Dorothy Popped a Few Pills)

Choosing subjects for a chapter on tortured artists and drug abuse presents its challenges. For one thing, drugs and alcohol feature prominently in the arts throughout most of history. The Greek dramatists loved their wine. Picasso's opium use influenced his Rose Period. And God only knows what Moby is on right now.

Although the difference between casual use and outright abuse is not always obvious, determining where such abuse falls in an artist's overall story arc is somewhat easier. Aldous Huxley recounted his experiences with mescaline for his 1954 nonfiction book, *The Doors of Perception*. Jim Morrison, whose rock group took its name from Huxley's book, often called upon his experiences with psychedelic drugs when he wrote song lyrics. But in contrasting the lives of these two wordsmiths, the difference between use and abuse becomes clear. Huxley lived to be sixty-nine. Morrison was found dead in a bathtub at the age of twenty-seven. For both, drug use began as earnest experimentation, but it was Morrison who crossed the line from dabbler to addict.

The following profiles feature tortured artists for whom drug and alcohol abuse overtook everything else in their lives. They are stories of lost potential, poor impulse control, and cravings run amok.

Jim Morrison

Judy Garland
(1922–1969)

Abstract: The view from way up high
Birth name: Frances Ethel Gumm
Birthplace: Grand Rapids, Minnesota, USA
Peak Performance: As Dorothy Gale in *The Wizard of Oz,* 1939
Demons: Uppers and downers

"I've sung. I've entertained. I've pleased your wives. I've pleased your children. I've pleased you—you sons of bitches."

—From a bootlegged recording of her unpublished memoirs, circa 1965

Some teenagers do drugs to rebel. Judy Garland was just doing what she was told. At fourteen, she was two years into a contract with MGM, tethered to a rigid studio system that dictated her little-girl image right down to her frilly bows and Peter Pan collars. In 1937, the *New York Post* referred to her as that "plump Judy Garland" in a review of one of her first movies, causing the studio to insist that she shed her baby fat at once. It would not be easy, however. Despite a studio-mandated diet of chicken soup and matzo balls, Judy was helpless against the beckoning of a very persistent sweet tooth. The actress would waste no opportunity to sneak off to Wil Wright's Ice Cream Parlor, on Hollywood Boulevard, where she would gorge herself on caramel sundaes doused in hot fudge. Such sugary excursions supplemented the secret stashes of candy and cookies she kept hidden in her dressing room. It got so bad that Louis B. Mayer, the head of MGM, held a meeting with other studio top brass to decide how Judy's waistline should best be dealt with.

Mayer, a neckless cigar-sucker who presided over the studio like a feisty Russian czar, was one of the first Hollywood producers to recognize the monetary value of movie stars, and he was determined to turn Judy into one. Protecting his investment in Judy meant keeping the girl trim at all costs, even if he had to shame the pounds off of her with insulting nicknames like "My Little Hunchback." At an age when girls are instinctively self-conscious of their bodies, Judy was plopped down in front of a mirror and compared to a plus-size mannequin. "Do you want to look like that dummy, or do you want to look like a star?" barked one MGM exec.

But a quick fix was on the horizon: a new drug called Benzedrine, which was becoming all the rage in Hollywood. Actors needed to suppress their appetites. Writers needed energy to work longer hours. It's no wonder this powerful amphetamine was seen as a miracle cure for all that ailed the movie industry. Consequently, no one really thought twice about loading Judy up on fistfuls of Bennies as a means of getting her to lose weight. It was an age of blind faith in medicine, a time when doctors were as quick with a prescription pad as they were with a golf swing. The drugs worked like a charm, melting the pounds from Judy's waistline like water on a witch. Granted, they had the unfortunate side effect of keeping her up all night, but the studio had a remedy for that as well: barbiturates. It was on this volatile cocktail of uppers and downers that Judy signed on for the movie role that would define her.

In 1937, Walt Disney Productions released *Snow White and the Seven Dwarfs*, the first feature-length animated movie, which shocked studio heads all over Hollywood by showing them that children's stories could mean big bucks at the box office. Mayer wanted in on the action as well, so in 1938, MGM bought the film rights to L. Frank Baum's 1900 children's book, *The Wonderful Wizard of Oz*, about a little girl named Dorothy who gets swept into a cyclone and transported to a magical land. Mayer thought Judy would make a perfect Dorothy, but there was a problem: At fifteen, she was developing the kind of curves that no amount of drug therapy could curb. Though the pills had apparently stunted her growth (she topped out at 4'11"), they could do nothing to hide other signs of Judy's impending womanhood. The studio's solution? Tape down her breasts and strap on a corset to flatten her curves. With her self-image already in tatters, Judy was now being forced to change her body again. She could not have known that she was about to star in a future classic—by some accounts the most watched movie of all time—nor would it have mattered. What mattered to the

"pumped full of pills before she was old enough to know better, Judy developed a lifelong habit that completely stifled any chance her career had at longevity"

seventeen-year-old girl was the insidious game of Whac-A-Mole being played with every growth spurt she went through. In creating a star, MGM damaged the person—for good.

The true extent of that damage finally came to a boil a decade later, when a scandal-happy rag called *Hollywood Nite Life* published a cover story about a young starlet whose personal life was being shattered by addiction. "Miss G," as the paper called her, had developed an incurable habit. She was a "pill-head," a victim of unscrupulous movie producers who were content to look the other way. While Judy's fans were shocked by the news, it came as no surprise to anyone in Hollywood. In the years since *The Wizard of Oz*, Judy had become a kind of local embarrassment, a mouth-foaming fiend who would beg for pills and raid medicine cabinets at parties. In 1950, less than two years after the news of her addiction went public, MGM canceled Judy's contract. The studio's official reason was unconvincingly altruistic: The termination was in "her own best interests." If nothing else, it was a consistent stance, as if all the years of pill pushing, breast taping, and ego bruising had been for the sake of building Judy's character. The truth—that MGM did not have the decency to clean up its own mess—would have been far more difficult to spin in a press statement.

As a tortured artist, Judy Garland belongs to an all-too-familiar genus: the tragic movie starlet whose self-esteem was shattered by an industry that chewed her up and spat her out. But she also stands as a quintessential example of an artist for whom substance abuse was less a consequence of her inner problems and more the cause of them. For that, we can no more blame her than we could a crack baby. Pumped full of pills before she was old enough to know better, Judy developed a lifelong habit that completely stifled any chance her career had at longevity. Pictures of the actress at forty-seven, a year before her death, may fool you into thinking she lived into her eighties. In an audio recording, which Judy intended as notes for her autobiography, the malaise of delirium and bitterness into which she descended became clear. "I am an angry lady," she rants. "I've been insulted, slandered, humiliated—but still America's sweetheart!" By the time Judy's fifth husband, Mickey Deans, found her dead in their London home, she had already been living "on borrowed time," according to her doctor, but her cirrhotic liver eventually had to give. In the world of substance abuse, it's not an uncommon ending. And yet, in Judy's case, it still feels particularly tragic, if only because her demise stood in such diametric opposition to the far-off rainbow over which her character once wished to fly. ～

Charlie Parker
(1920–1955)

Abstract: Bop till you drop dead
Birth name: Charles Parker Jr.
Birthplace: Kansas City, Kansas, USA
Peak Performance: With "The Quintet," Massey Hall, Toronto, 1953
Demons: The rumors and realities of dope

"Some of these smart kids who think you have to be completely knocked out to be a good horn man are just plain crazy. It's not true. I know, believe me."
—Interview with *Down Beat* magazine, 1949

Charlie Parker was first introduced to heroin at the age of fifteen, either by a childhood friend or a stranger in a men's bathroom, depending on how he recalled the story. The details of that first fix may have been fuzzy, but the immense gratification it provided was always in the front of his mind. With one prick of a needle, the struggling high school student whose father had recently abandoned him felt his problems instantly evaporate in a warm flood of orgasmic tingles. And from the very first moment he rose into that ethereal weightlessness, Charlie knew he never wanted to come down.

"You mean there's something like *this* in the world?" he asked, digging into his pockets and pulling out his last dollar. "How much will this buy me?" What it bought him, of course, was a lifetime of instability and dependence, which followed him through his rise to the top of the jazz world as well as the rapid fall that followed his success.

Despite his reputation as one of the most innovative horn men in jazz history, Charlie Parker showed little aptitude for musical greatness in his early years. In fact, some of his first attempts to showcase his talents ended in outright humiliation. At the age of sixteen, the eager young saxophone player entered a competitive jam session at the Kansas City jazz nightery the Reno Club, where he hoped to make a positive impression on Count Basie and his band. Unfortunately, those aging jazz greats had grown to believe that the sun rises and sets around musical precision, and Parker was no expert in jazz theory. He had a lot of youthful energy, but he lacked technical ability. When it came time for his solo, Charlie fumbled, evoking critical scowls from everyone in the club. Basie's drummer, Jo Jones,

"with one prick of a needle, the struggling high school student whose father had recently abandoned him felt his problems instantly evaporate in a warm flood of orgasmic tingles"

so objected to Parker's playing that he sneaked up behind him and threw his cymbal on the floor. The deafening crash marked Parker as a clumsy greenhorn who couldn't cut it with the pros, and the discouraged youngster packed up his sax and stormed out in a huff. "I'll get 'em," he vowed. "They rang a bell on me. I'll get 'em!"

And he did. Over the next three years, Charlie Parker—nicknamed "Bird" for his love of chicken—spent nearly every waking hour learning his instrument, training his fingers to perform with the all-fierce exactitude that jazz demanded. By the end of the 1930s, he had moved to New York City, where he could hold his own among the most skillful players in the country. In fact, he had gotten so good that conventional jam sessions were now leaving him bored. "I kept thinking there's bound to be something else," he said. "I could hear it sometimes, but I couldn't play it."

In 1939, during a jam session at Dan Wall's Chili House, in Harlem, Charlie discovered a solution to the tedium by hitting on higher intervals within standard chord progressions. It was the first time that his fingers pulled off the meta-melodies that he had been hearing in his head, and the resulting chord changes would form the foundation of a complex new style of jazz called *bebop*. Charlie Parker, once shamed by pedantic players for being musically illiterate, had rewritten the language.

If Charlie's story had ended there, it might have made for a nice little apologue about one man's ability to realize his potential. But Charlie never realized his potential, mainly because when he wasn't out revolutionizing the music world, he was shagging the insatiable cravings of his first love. That first shot of heroin at the age of fifteen gave him a taste for something that had no substitute.

Charlie's dedication to his instrument, steadfast as it was, often did not supersede his temptation to pawn his saxophone for a helping of smack. He became notorious for his unreliability, repeatedly getting himself thrown out of bands for missing gigs or nodding off on stage. In 1946, he lit his Los Angeles hotel room on fire, was arrested while wandering around in a drug-induced stupor, and was later incarcerated at Camarillo State Mental Hospital. It was the first of three such institutional incarcerations for Charlie, the last of which followed two suicide attempts and the death of his infant daughter, Pree, which only pushed him further into the throes of addiction. Perhaps more troubling to Charlie than heroin itself was the undercurrent of mythologists who kept insisting that his drug of choice was partially responsible for his genius, a rumor that deeply embedded dope into bebop culture. Charlie, aware of his role in that myth, did what he could to dispel it.

"Any musician who says he is playing better [on heroin] is a plain, straight liar," he complained. Meanwhile, such stereotypes stifled broader acceptance of bebop. Mainstream critics who couldn't wrap their heads around the music simply dismissed it as the screechy noise of junked-out black guys. And yet, despite such pans, bebop was inspiring a decidedly white counterculture, fronted by skinny young cats in goatees and pork pie hats. Bebop improvisation also captivated figures from Jack Kerouac to Woody Allen, who understood it as a type of jazz that demanded intellectual commitment from the listener. These were not danceable jazz anthems performed by big bands in concert halls but personal expressions by impassioned artists.

For Charlie Parker, that personal expression was one of defenselessness against a substance that, piece by piece, tore his body to shreds. Later in life, debilitated by chronic pain, he thought it ironic that expensive doctors could do nothing

Card Games

In 1951, Charlie Parker, by then notorious for rampant drug and alcohol use, had his New York City Cabaret Card revoked, barring him from playing any nightclub in the city that served liquor. He was not alone. The cards, instituted after prohibition and used until 1967, were a kind of witch-hunting tool for city officials who believed they could muscle troublemaking musicians out of town. Among other musicians of the era who had their cards revoked were Chet Baker, Thelonious Monk, and Billie Holiday, all for drug-related charges. One performer who would not play the city's game, however, was Frank Sinatra. Rather than submit to the lengthy application process, which he found demeaning, Old Blue Eyes came up with his own solution: He simply refused to perform in New York.

for him while a $5 bag purchased in an alleyway could still make his pain disappear. And if Charlie's self-destruction can be summed up in any particular moment of poignancy, that moment came in 1955, when his erratic behavior got him banned from Birdland, the midtown jazz club named after him. It was a few months later, at the Stanhope Hotel on the Upper East Side, that Charlie stopped breathing while watching TV. Which of his major organs was the first to give way is anyone's guess, as they were all pretty much shot. Even the coroner who performed the autopsy was stumped, estimating Charlie's thirty-four-year-old body to be between fifty and sixty years old. ∿

John Belushi
(1949–1982)

Abstract: Voted least likely to survive
Birth name: John Adam Belushi
Birthplace: Chicago, Illinois, USA
Peak Performance: The first three seasons of *Saturday Night Live*
Demons: Instant gratification

"I guess happiness is not a state you want to be in all the time."
    —**Interview with *Cosmopolitan* magazine, 1981**

Long before DVRs freed us from the rigid airtimes of our favorite shows, conventional wisdom maintained that very few people enjoyed television enough to stay home and watch it on a Saturday night. So when NBC tapped Lorne Michaels to fill that shunned time slot, the twenty-eight-year-old writer banked on the hope that not even Peacock censors would be tuning in to see what he came up with. Hoping to create something truly edgy, Lorne began scouring the clubs and theaters of New York City for risqué young talent. He soon stumbled upon a stage show by National Lampoon Inc., helmed by a hilarious troupe of spoofsters whose roster included such performers as Chevy Chase and Gilda Radner.

It was pretty much all the talent Lorne needed. One by one, he signed the Lampooners for his new sketch-comedy program, but when he sat down with John Belushi—a manic, intense scene-stealer who seemed to lack even the slightest trace of inhibition—the meeting didn't go so smoothly. "My television has spit all over it," John blurted, effectively ending the conversation before it started.

For John, acting was an interactive sport, meaningless without the immediate feedback of a live audience. Born and raised in Chicago, where improvisational comedy trumps Shakespeare on the theatrical totem pole, the actor cut his teeth working with the legendary improv troupe Second City. Although he later became known for ingesting enough drugs to violate the Geneva Protocol's provisions on chemical warfare, John, as a younger man, preferred instant gratification of a more natural grade. Howling laughter and raucous applause gave him a blissful rush, keeping his feet on a stage and his TV covered in saliva. As he insisted to Lorne, he had no use for a medium so steeped in sterility and solitude. What John did not realize, however, was just how well the late-night program would mesh with his anti-TV stance. The show would be edgy, unapologetic. It would embrace controversial humor and mock current events. Most of all, though, it would air live—something TV audiences hadn't seen since the fifties. John, after repeated goading from his fellow Lampooners, reluctantly joined the cast of *Saturday Night Live*. He was so torn by the decision, in fact, that he refused to sign his contract until the day of the first airing, October 11, 1975, mere months before he would emerge as the quintessential Not Ready for Prime-Timer, only to morph into one of the fastest-living cautionary tales of the live-fast-die-young seventies.

But it was John's addiction to the rush of audience praise that fueled his performances. His stage work, as well as his first few seasons on *SNL*, provided the fix he needed. But by the time he signed on to *SNL*, the natural highs provided by his audiences were dangerously supplemented by a potpourri of mind-altering chemicals. (In one early *SNL* screen test, John can already be seen sniffing his way through an entire four minutes of Brando impressions and eyebrow exercises.) Drugs had not yet seized control of John's life, but then the $750 a week he received as an *SNL* cast member did not exactly leave room for overindulgence.

That would soon change. In 1978, John catapulted from *SNL* into the American crass-consciousness as Bluto, the beer-guzzling cretin of *National Lampoon's Animal House*, which became the top comedy of the year. (Gross-out masters from the Farrelly brothers to Judd Apatow can thank their careers to John's potato-spitting imitation of a zit.) By the following year, John had the number-one late-night television show, the top-selling album on the *Billboard* charts, and the highest-grossing comedy in cinema history. Now wealthy enough to afford any cocktail of drugs his overtaxed heart desired, he alternated between rampant binges and hiring bodyguards to help keep him from using.

John, as his coworkers routinely noted, had no off switch. Unfortunately, moviegoers did.

"now wealthy enough to afford any cocktail of drugs his overtaxed heart desired, he alternated between rampant binges and hiring bodyguards to help keep him from using"

They cooled significantly to his antics by 1981, when he tried to pass himself off as a romantic lead in the flop *Continental Divide*. His screen cred slipped even further with his next film, *Neighbors*, which would also be his last. That movie's oddly counterintuitive story line had John playing straight man to a wacky Dan Aykroyd, a device that made it feel like a reject from the body-switch genre popularized by *Freaky Friday*.

With his movie career in shambles, John decided to take matters into his own hands and write his own film, *Noble Rot*—a comedy set in wine country, which he hoped would help him reclaim his Bluto glory. The truth was he had already strayed too far from his live-comedy roots. Whereas his work once produced the instantly gratifying feedback of enthusiastic applause, it now produced jeers from film critics and indifference from Paramount execs, who were unimpressed by early drafts of *Noble Rot*.

John's all-or-nothing performance style took him from intimate off-Broadway stages to the recesses of the Chateau Marmont, on the Sunset Strip, where he spent his final days hammering out rewrites and partying with Robin Williams.

On March 5, 1982, a partygoer at John's bungalow injected him with the speedball that ended his life at the age of thirty-three. The woman eventually served a fifteen-month prison sentence for involuntary manslaughter.

In a recent interview with the Associated Press, Dan Aykroyd imagined what John would be doing today had he survived the early eighties: He would have given up movies, according to his *Blues Brothers* costar, and returned to the stage. The prospect of an old-and-gray John Belushi recalls the famous *SNL* sketch "Don't Look Back in Anger," in which John plays himself as an old man, visiting—and dancing on—the graves of his former cast mates. The irony, of course, is that John had already been voted the least likely to survive. If the sketch seems less funny in retrospect, it helps to know that John himself was in on the joke, even if it was at his own expense. Anything for a laugh. And a rush. ∿

Heath Ledger
(1979–2008)

Abstract: Sleep no more
Birth name: Heath Andrew Ledger
Birthplace: Perth, Australia
Peak Performance: As Ennis Del Mar in *Brokeback Mountain*, 2005
Demons: Being under the microscope

"I love acting. Oh, God, I love it. But all this fame and all this bullshit attention. I'm not supernatural. I've done nothing extremely special to deserve the position."
—Interview with *Newsweek* magazine, 2000

Executives at Sony Pictures Entertainment had a plan for Heath Ledger: They were going to turn him into a teen heartthrob. In 2001, shortly before the release of *A Knight's Tale*, Sony bigwigs sat down for a meeting with the film's twenty-two-year-old leading man to discuss promotional strategies. Everyone agreed that Heath exhibited just the right combination of dangerous charm and nontoxic good looks—an edgy rock star with a little Doogie Howser thrown in for good measure. But *A Knight's Tale* was his first starring role in a Hollywood movie, and the campaign to promote it would need to be aggressive. Heath would have to tour the country. He would have to appear in malls and at video stores, posing for photo ops under movie posters bearing the tag line, "He will rock you!" However, what sounded like *Tiger Beat* gold to Sony sounded like a nightmare to Heath. He never finished the meeting that day. Panicked by the thought of press junkets and publicity tours, he leapt from the table, darted out of the room, and locked himself in a bathroom stall.

Anyone familiar with Heath Ledger's trajectory after the success of *A Knight's Tale* knows that his career ended abruptly. Less than seven years later, he was found dead in his SoHo loft from a toxic combination of Xanax, Valium, Vicodin, OxyContin, and cold medicine. The Australian actor did not become the blond-haired heartthrob that Sony execs had hoped, nor did he circumvent the scrutiny and idolatry he wished to avoid. Instead, his short time in the spotlight was undone by an age-old actor-as-artist paradox, in which the need for notoriety clashes with the desire for anonymity.

"he was found dead in his SoHo loft from a toxic combination of Xanax, Valium, Vicodin, OxyContin, and cold medicine"

Heath once called himself an "illusionist." An actor's job, he believed, was not just to dive into a role but to completely disappear within it. He realized this acting philosophy most fully in 2004, when he signed on to play the closed-off and closeted Ennis Del Mar in *Brokeback Mountain*. Ang Lee's willfully contemplative indie drama followed a secret love affair between two ranchmen in 1960s Wyoming, but what began as a project of dubious commercial appeal— "the gay cowboy movie," as casual observers called it—seeped into the mainstream. At the center of the film's universal appeal was Heath's performance. His subtle, Brando-esque mumbling brought Ennis's hopeless longing into delicate fruition. *Brokeback* went on to be the most honored movie of 2005, propelling Heath to the forefront of awards season with an Oscar nod for best actor. For Heath, winning an Oscar meant the freedom to take on even more challenging roles. However, going for the brass ring involved paying a steep price, at least for the publicity-averse Heath. It meant more of everything he despised—more events, more photo ops. The whole effort amounted to an artless political campaign, jumping in the fray and joining the ranks of would-be Oscar winners as they clamored for the attention of Academy voters. Nevertheless, Heath played the game for the promise of Oscar gold.

"He really did whore himself around, doing all the things he hated," Terry Gilliam, who directed Heath in *The Imaginarium of Doctor Parnassus*, told *Vanity Fair* magazine. "He felt angry with himself for going along with the way the system worked. He felt dirty." If the debasing process of "For Your Consideration" crusades made Heath feel dirty, then perhaps it's fitting that he took a bath in the race for statuette glory, losing to Philip Seymour Hoffman's helium-voiced take on Truman Capote.

Hollywood politics may have left Heath with a bitter taste in his mouth, but they would be nothing compared to the treatment he would receive in his native Australia, where swarms of pestering paparazzi badgered him right off the continent. Uncomfortable with his growing fame, Heath reacted with more and more hostility toward the throngs of snappers and shooters who followed him around constantly. The Australian press, not unlike those fifth graders who discover that they can get a rise out of you by flicking your ears on the school bus, simply grew more emboldened by Heath's agitation. At the Sydney premiere of *Brokeback Mountain*, Heath stepped onto the red carpet only to be squirted with water pistols by several photographers. The incident left Heath in tears, according to his father, who said the actor called him that night to tell him he was selling his beachside Sydney home and relocating to Brooklyn—permanently.

Heath fostered equal enmity for those on the highest and lowest rungs of the showbiz ladder: the bigwigs who tried to polish his image and the bottom feeders who wanted to make a buck selling candid photos to tabloids. It's rather appropriate that his anarchistic take on the Joker, in 2008's *The Dark Knight,* was partially inspired by the former Sex Pistol Johnny Rotten, who was spitting vodka at record executives before Heath was born. It was during preparations for that role that the incurable insomnia that would lead to Heath's demise began to overtake his life. Heath was averaging two hours' sleep a night when he sequestered himself in a hotel room for a month, writing down what he imagined might be the deranged thoughts of his sociopathic character. He tried popping a few Ambien pills, but the effects of that drug scarcely lasted an hour before he'd wake up again to find his mind still racing.

The true extent of Heath's drug use has been obscured behind conflicting reports by the people who knew him. Personal accounts of Heath's behavior range from stories of the actor snorting piles of cocaine to testimonies from those who claim they'd never seen him with anything stronger than a cigarette. Regardless of which version is closer to reality, one thing is clear: Heath's plunge into substance abuse was an act of desperation—a last-ditch coping mechanism by a tortured young man who needed relief from a brain that would not turn off. Whether it was a run-in with a paparazzo or throwing himself into a new role, the everyday stressors of movie-star life fueled his tendency to think too much. That tendency only worsened after he separated from his partner, the actress Michelle Williams, who later recalled how Heath's overactive mind was always "turning, turning, turning."

After his breakup in late 2007, Heath took up residence in Manhattan's SoHo neighborhood. It was only a few months later that he turned up dead at the age of twenty-eight. Whether posthumous kismet or plain old irony, his death came only a short time before major promotions were to begin for *The Dark Knight*, casting a fable-like shadow over the film's release that helped make it the most successful picture of the year. In February 2009, Heath Ledger won an Oscar for his role as the Joker, beating out Phillip Seymour Hoffman (for *Doubt*) and becoming only the second actor in history to win the award posthumously. He didn't have to appear in a single photo op to get it. ～

Amy Winehouse
(1983–2011)

Abstract: Chasing Amy's tail
Birth name: Amy Jade Winehouse
Birthplace: London, England
Masterwork: *Back to Black*
Demons: Addiction and violence

"I write songs because I'm fucked up in the head and need to get something good out of something bad."
—Interview with *Spin* magazine, 2007

On June 14, 2007, Amy Winehouse graced the cover of *Rolling Stone* magazine for the first and only time during her brief career. The cover photo is a head-and-shoulders shot of the terminally troubled songstress donning all of the attributes we have come to associate with her: the cat-eye makeup, the pinup-girl tattoos, the pouty sneer. The magazine's familiar logo is obscured by Amy's towering hairdo, while the headline below promises a revealing exposé of "The Diva and Her Demons." Among the apparent revelations in the story is that Amy was booted out of London's Sylvia Young Theatre School for getting her nose pierced and displaying a generally combative attitude. At thirteen, the future queen of neo-soul was already a rebel, which is just the kind of colorful past we would expect from the singer whose drug-addled life made "Rehab" one of the most ironically titled songs in history.

The *Rolling Stone* article, like Amy herself, fulfilled a promise to a train-wreck-loving public who had come to view her foibles as just another form of home entertainment. Never mind that Sylvia Young later denied that Amy was expelled from her school. The story, true or not, fits too perfectly into Amy's fractured image. When the singer became the latest member of the 27 Club on July 23, 2011, her untimely death confirmed her apparent determination to live out the Oliver Stone–directed version of her own life.

And yet Amy's transformation from a promising soul singer to the tabloid cartoon who tumbled out of bars, punched fans in the face, and toked on mysterious pipes would scarcely be a biopic in the making had she not also produced one of the defining albums of the aimless aughts. *Back to Black,* Amy's 2006 smash hit, was a rarified pop-culture phenomenon in the à-la-carte age of iTunes. A spirited throwback to sixties soul, it was fitted with the heart of a modern-day tigress and seasoned with just enough minstrelsy flare to qualify as an homage without coming off as racist.

Back to Black came into being as the direct result of Amy's violent relationship with Blake Fielder-Civil, the lanky video-production assistant who is often blamed for introducing her to heroin, crack, and other assorted substances.

In 2005, Amy was still coasting on the U.K. success of her first album, *Frank*, which, if nothing else, lived up to its title. Released in 2003, *Frank* was a solid okay—elevator music by way of a porn soundtrack, topped off by Amy's buttery voice and snarky ruminations. But two years after the album's release, the singer had shown little interest in writing a follow-up. As one A&R ("artist and repertoire") rep for Island Records said of the twenty-one-year-old Amy, "She just didn't have the subject matter to write about. She needed to live it first." As if following that advice to the letter, Amy "lived it" through her relationship with Blake, a destructive, on-again-off-again freak show made all too combustible by the forces of media attention. Ostensibly, Amy and Blake's coupling was a familiar trope: the rock-star rebel and the groupie who latched on for a slice of the glamour—Sid and Nancy in reverse, as it were. Amy had his name tattooed over her left breast and once carved the words "I Love Blake" on her abdomen with a shard of mirror, apparently hoping to shock a journalist. British tabloids vilified Blake, placing responsibility for Amy's downward spiral almost solely in his boney lap. But Amy stood by her man.

"a destructive, on-again-off-again freak show made all too combustible by the forces of media attention"

Consider the night they were both discovered at London's swanky Sanderson Hotel, bruised and bloody, as if they had just beaten each other to a pulp. Amy later claimed that she harmed herself. Blake, she said, would never lay a finger on her.

Whichever version you believe, there is no mistaking that the brutal energy infusing their relationship was the very thing that made *Back to Black* the force it became. Written during a period when the two had broken up, the songs are an account of scorned love and subsequent self-pity. (The title track recounts how Amy drowned herself in mind-altering chemicals after Blake refused to leave his other girlfriend.) *Back to Black* was released in October 2006. By mid-2007, "Rehab" was shooting up the *Billboard* charts and Amy and Blake were on again. The couple married in May of that year. "Here is a song I wrote when he left me a couple years ago," she said, introducing the ubiquitous hit during a Los Angeles radio performance. "I wrote the whole album about it, really. We went on our little separate ways, and then realized that we loved each other. Life's too short."

That last line, of course, became far more poignant once the singer was found dead, but her life with Blake would be shorter than she realized. After attacking a London club owner, Blake was sent to prison in 2008, and although the couple divorced in 2009, Amy never seemed to fully give him up. Just months before her death, she was reportedly firing off alcohol-induced texts to her ex, whose new fiancée publicly complained of the spaced-out messages in which Amy signed off as "your wife."

Meanwhile, rehab clinics throughout the London area had all but installed revolving doors to accommodate her comings and goings, and when she tried to stay clean enough to perform, she would often slur through a set just long enough to be booed off stage. Her worst moments always seemed to be captured for posterity by smart phone–wielding spectators who were determined to turn Amy into the first tortured artist whose downfall was documented real-time via YouTube.

The novelty factor for modern rock rebels is, admittedly, difficult to sustain. The music world has seen more of its share of Amy Wine-houses over the last half century. And given the brevity of her pop reign, her legacy will most certainly face challenges as less destructive, Gaga-style rabble-rousers take her place. Hanging in the balance are both Amy's artistry and her circus act: Is she a Gen-Y Kurt Cobain or a female Andy Kaufman? Only hindsight will allow a verdict. But for anyone who just started paying attention after they carried her body out of that London flat, yes, she really meant all that "no, no, no" stuff. ∽

8

Archetypes

Touchstones of the Touched

Four people—an actress, a writer, a musician, a painter—have not only lived up to tortured-artist folklore but helped define it: Marilyn, the lost starlet; Plath, the suicidal poet; Cobain, the angsty rock star; van Gogh, the delusional Post-Impressionist. We know their tragic stories well. And yet, despite the fact that their personal demons have themselves become part of the vast repository of pop provincialism, their legacies as artists have not been eclipsed.

In researching the lives of these four—let's call them the Dream Team—what is most striking are the many similarities among them. None lived past the age of forty, and each died amid fuzzy circumstances that were ultimately ruled suicides. Moreover, it's impossible not to notice the role that mental illness played in each of their lives. Each experienced bursts of euphoric energy followed by crippling depression.

However, the aim of this chapter is not to make the case that these artists shared the same mental condition, nor is it to dispel the many myths and misunderstandings that surround their lives. The aim is to show how the archetype of the tortured artist played out in the lives of these four troubled souls, each of whom took the gamble of choosing art over safety. Marilyn left behind a perfectly safe marriage to seek out Hollywood. Sylvia exposed her worst enemies in a thinly veiled novel. Kurt ditched underground success for a chance to change the direction of mainstream music. Vincent traded any semblance of security to live in poverty as a painter. In these instances, all four of these figures showed that they were willing to risk everything for their art. Can there be a truer definition of an artist?

Marilyn Monroe
(1926–1962)

Abstract: Color me blonde
Birth name: Norma Jeane Mortenson
Birthplace: Los Angeles, California, USA
Peak Performance: On the subway grate in *The Seven Year Itch*, 1955
Demons: Us

"When you are famous every weakness is exaggerated."
—**Final interview, *LIFE* magazine, 1962**

Try to picture Marilyn Monroe as an old lady, and chances are you will come up blank. Her public image of the willing but woozy blonde hinged upon the illusion that sexuality is inextricably linked with childlike innocence. It was an illusion that Marilyn made completely believable, at least to every male in the country, but it wasn't without its limits. On August 5, 1962, the day that Marilyn was found dead in her Brentwood home from an apparent barbiturate overdose, the illusion had already been in danger for some time, threatened by the rapidly approaching expiration date of Marilyn's human half, a mere mortal named Norma Jeane, who at thirty-six was only four years away from the mandatory retirement age of Hollywood leading ladies. As for Marilyn, Norma Jeane's platinum alter ego, she had been slipping further and further out of control, so hopped up on prescription drugs that she could barely remember her lines. Her unreliability had halted production on her latest film, *Something's Got to Give*, a George Cukor comedy whose title now seems an eerily prophetic reference to the mental instability of its star.

In effect, Marilyn Monroe had reached that all-too-common showbiz breaking point at which an untimely death appears to be the best of all possible career moves. Who better than she to open a chapter about archetypes? Marilyn, like the wax figure of her at Madame Tussauds, is timeless—and ageless—by design.

This is not to suggest that uncovering Marilyn the tortured artist is easy. For a life whose every detail has been scrutinized, piecing together a consistent picture of her personal demons is about as likely as solving the Israeli-Palestinian conflict with a coin toss. In the fifty years since her death, Marilyn has been defined and redefined by countless pundits who insist that she is more than a screen goddess, or a tragic victim of fame, or a detached Gemini, or a coffee mug. And while Norman Mailer once called her "every man's love affair with America," it was Gloria Steinem who, perhaps more astutely, called her a "frightened child of the past." Scratch the surface of that past and you will discover the rootless underpinnings of someone who will inevitably need attention in the same way that the rest of us need air.

She was born to an unknown father and a paranoid-schizophrenic mother, who spent most of her life in sanitariums. Her grandmother, too, was institutionalized, and she died in an asylum. As a child, Marilyn was shuffled between different foster homes. At sixteen, the age of consent, she got married to a man she hardly knew just so she could avoid another orphanage. The marriage, it goes without saying, was loveless and sexually unsatisfying. It was also the final straw that compelled her to seek out the glamour of Hollywood.

Norma—and consequently Marilyn—lived in constant fear that she would one day unravel the same way her mother and grandmother did. Marilyn always believed that her days of mental clarity might be numbered, and she had plenty of reason to. It was in her teens that she began to hear voices and conjure up imaginary stalkers. As her fame grew, she wedged more and more distance between the frightened girl who feared insanity and the flirty blond movie star she created. Obscured by the bleach and pencil skirts was, we're told, a brainy thing who enjoyed the poetry of Keats and the theories of Freud, but that person is nowhere to be found in her onscreen performances, nor is her desire to be taken seriously as an actress.

"she had been slipping further and further out of control, so hopped up on prescription drugs that she could barely remember her lines"

Marilyn said that her ultimate artistic wish was to perform Shakespeare, but she never fulfilled that dream. The immutability of the Marilyn mystique was too rigid for anyone to have accepted her as a breathy-voiced Ophelia, and the existential prison of her identity caused the actress greater and greater distress. Toward the end of her life, when a star-struck fan, mouth agape, looked at her and asked if she was *really* Marilyn Monroe, Marilyn replied, "I guess I am. Everybody says I am."

The year before Marilyn's death, her psychoanalyst was convinced that the actress was suicidal—so much so that she had her committed to New York's Payne Whitney Psychiatric Clinic. Encouraged to go to the hospital for "rest and relaxation," Marilyn suddenly found herself locked in a padded room. She broke down, crying and shouting to be released, pounding on the steel door until her fists were bleeding. "I'm locked up with these poor nutty people," Marilyn wrote in a letter to Lee Strasberg and his wife. "I'm sure to end up a nut, too, if I stay in this nightmare. Please help me." It took Joltin' Joe DiMaggio to bail her out, despite the fact that the two had already been divorced for six years. One phone call from his ex, and the former Yankee Clipper was on a plane from Florida. He stormed into the hospital, demanded to see his wife, and then had her transferred to Columbia Presbyterian, where she remained for three weeks.

Health problems prevented Marilyn from working until the following year, when she signed on to star in the Cukor picture she would never finish. By the time she was found dead, Cukor, fed up with her unreliability, had already tried to have her replaced. Marilyn's death was ruled a "probable suicide," but conspiracy theories of murder abound. One of the most prevailing murder theories places the blame on us—that is, her voracious public, who would not have tolerated seeing her reach the age of forty. It falls in line with the blank head one gets when trying to picture Marilyn as an old lady. The notion that Marilyn's untimely death was in compliance with our desire to turn her into an ageless icon is one of the more unsettling myths that surround her life. Even more unsettling, of course, is the possibility that it might not be a myth at all. ~

Sylvia Plath
(1932–1963)

Abstract: The art of dying slowly
Birth name: Sylvia Plath
Birthplace: Boston, Massachusetts, USA
Masterwork: *The Bell Jar*
Demons: The future

"I shall perish if I can write about no one but myself."
—From a journal entry, 1959

One does not typically associate Sylvia Plath with happy endings. The famously tortured confessional poet has been synonymous with suffering since her calculated suicide set into motion an endless cycle of sulky enchantment—usually beginning in high school, when girls discover her poetry and boys discover girls who discover her poetry. However, amid the dour lore of oven-baked matrons and posthumously published laments, it's easy to forget that *The Bell Jar*, Plath's only novel and by most accounts her signature work, ends on a willfully hopeful note. After plodding through disastrous relationships, a dreadful internship at a prominent women's magazine, and a stint in a mental institution, Esther Greenwood—the novel's Plath-by-proxy protagonist—enters her final psychiatric evaluation with a renewed sense of herself and her place in the world. The results of her evaluation are never revealed, and yet the intentional uncertainty gives us no indication that Esther will end up as her real-life counterpart ultimately did. This was the real tragedy of Sylvia Plath, a still-developing writer, teetering on the brink of madness, who might have gone on to produce a body of work extensive enough to liberate her from her own cult status.

Despite Sylvia's image as the long-suffering poet, her New England girlhood was marked by focused ambition and unrivaled academic prowess, making it all the more tempting to ask what went so horribly wrong.

"the famously tortured confessional poet has been synonymous with suffering since her calculated suicide set into motion an endless cycle of sulky enchantment"

In junior high she was already writing for school periodicals. She was coeditor of her high school newspaper, and she had a story published in *Seventeen* magazine when she was actually seventeen. On a scholarship, she attended the ruthlessly selective Smith College, where she became the editor of *The Smith Review*, and in her third year, she landed the coveted guest editorship at *Mademoiselle* magazine, which would serve as the setting for *The Bell Jar*. It was during that experience, however, that her perpetually upward trajectory took a sharp turn.

In the summer of 1953, Sylvia spent a month in New York City with nineteen other students to put out a special college issue of *Mademoiselle*. But what seemed like a dream opportunity quickly descended into a demanding and demoralizing affair. Sylvia, like the fictional Esther, suffered under the dictates of a whip-cracking editor who, if slightly less Wintourian than Meryl Streep's fire-breathing editrix in *The Devil Wears Prada*, was abrupt enough to shake Sylvia's proud-Smith-girl confidence with constant critiques of her performance. Meanwhile, the grueling office hours she was required to keep were followed by exhausting late-night parties and press functions—the types of activities expected of trendsetting socialites in the magazine world. Through it all, Sylvia found herself growing to resent the New Yorky elitism espoused by her colleagues, all while trying to ensure that her academic career would serve as more than a pit stop to the traditional path of marriage and suburban schmuckdom.

Sylvia returned home, disillusioned with journalism, only to find that academia, her old standby, might be shutting her out as well. She was denied acceptance into an esteemed writing class at Harvard, and for the first time, the academic superstar was facing the deflating realization that she was not, as she had once maintained, chosen by fate to live the life of a writer. As the possibility of a truncated college career loomed, she attempted to learn shorthand—an administrative skill to fall back on—but being unable to master "those senseless curlicues" left her even more frustrated. For the next month, she subsisted on almost no sleep, and methods of suicide began to plague her every thought. After cutting up her legs with razor blades "just to see if she had the guts," Sylvia was hospitalized and given electroconvulsive therapy. But the procedure only jolted her into a premeditated decision to end her life, once and for all. As she later wrote to her pen pal, "The only alternative I could see was an eternity of hell for the rest of my life in a mental institution."

The image of the nineteen-year-old Sylvia squeezing herself into a crawl space under her porch, popping sleeping pills one by one, will be vividly familiar to readers of *The Bell Jar*. In the book, she recounts that moment of desperation with an almost romantic eagerness to unburden Esther from the weightiness of her life. In fact, for Sylvia, the novel was as much a catharsis as a creative endeavor—completed eight years after the fact by an older, wiser Sylvia who was committed to unloading the baggage of her youth. The book so closely mirrored her real-life experiences that she published it under a pseudonym, hoping to avoid confrontations with those whom she unflatteringly portrayed. She also hoped that *The Bell Jar* would signal her transition from poet to novelist, but obstacles prohibiting that transition surfaced almost immediately—beginning with the reception of the book itself. American publishers rejected the novel, dismissing its story line as melodramatic and unrealistic. (One editor said of Sylvia's protagonist, "I was not at all prepared as a reader to accept the extent of her illness.") Even today the book struggles with perception issues. That Meg Griffin is seen reading it in an episode of *Family Guy* is not exactly an endorsement. When *The Bell Jar* was published in the United Kingdom, in January 1963, reviews were tepid at best, with one critic advising his readers to "stick to home produce." What the critics did not know, however, was that they were debasing the work of a very disturbed writer who would be dead within a matter of weeks. Quite frankly, one only needs to revisit Esther's assessment of her own self-pitying inklings: "Wherever I sat—on the deck of a ship or at a street café in Paris or Bangkok, I would be sitting under the same glass bell jar, stewing in my own sour air."

Of course, this is the Sylvia Plath that attracts readers such as Meg Griffin. It's the moribund heroine, obsessed with her own suffering. It's the Sylvia Plath of *Ariel*, her final collection of poems, in which she bitterly tackles each of her life's disappointments: her father's death when she was eight, her conflicted feelings about motherhood, the philandering of her husband, Ted Hughes. Although the poems are the most defining of her career, she would not live to see them published. On the morning of February 11, 1963, she placed her head in the oven and cranked the gas to full blast. Like so many tales of tortured artists, the event, in retrospect, seems as if it were predestined for the annals of cult culture. But as Sylvia so clearly conveyed in *The Bell Jar*'s final scene, as her protagonist likens her ordeal to a second birth, a happy ending would have been a far more preferable outcome. ∾

Kurt Cobain
(1967–1994)

Abstract: The unbearable lightness
Birth name: Kurt Donald Cobain
Birthplace: Hoquiam, Washington, USA
Masterwork: *Nevermind*
Demons: Anonymity and fame

"I can't work among people. I may as well try and make a career out of this."
—Interview with *Sounds* magazine, 1990

For anyone who grew up fascinated by the tales of ill-fated musicians, the story of Kurt Cobain is almost too perfect: A reluctant rock star, tortured by fame, senselessly blows his own brains out at the height of his career. The tragedy seemed to borrow from every rock 'n' roll fable that had come before it, only this time it was being repackaged to fit that decade of disaffection known as the 1990s. Cobain, the contradictory mouthpiece for a generation tired of mouthpieces, borrowed from the very rule book he claimed to hate. And yet if his destructive-rock-star persona was really a postmodernist wink to dead-at-twenty-seven icons like Jimi Hendrix and Jim Morrison, then his final act would have to make us wonder: Was he as tortured as he claimed to be, or did he simply play out a self-fulfilling cliché of rock stardom?

Kurt's demons began as the attention-seeking cries of a typical latchkey kid only to devolve into the concentrated, careful-what-you-wish-for morality tale that followed his mainstream success. However, his tendency to lash out at the world did not begin with the runaway success of "Smells Like Teen Spirit." Growing up under the perpetual cloud cover of Aberdeen, Washington, in the early 1970s, Kurt was the Dennis the Menace of his sleepy neighborhood— a golden-haired terror who ran wild in the streets, banged on pots and pans, sang Beatles songs, jumped his bicycle like Evel Knievel, and basically drove everybody crazy.

"a reluctant rock star, tortured by fame, senselessly blows his own brains out at the height of his career"

He was eventually diagnosed with Attention Deficit Disorder, one of the hot new pediatric maladies for the Count Chocula generation, and he was subsequently prescribed Ritalin at the age of seven. As Kurt recalled it, however, his so-called hyperactivity was simply a case of misinterpreted bliss. "I was an extremely happy child," he told biographer Michael Azerrad. "I was always screaming and singing. I didn't know when to quit."

Two years later, when his parents told him they were getting divorced, Kurt's insular world was shattered. He later blamed the breakup of his cozy nuclear unit for a subsequent descent into insolence and alienation, a downward spiral from which he never bounced back. His kinetic energy was still there, but it was intermittent, tempered by severe mood swings that followed the loud-quiet-loud pattern now familiar to even the most casual Nirvana listener. By the time Kurt reached high school, however, being isolated in such an isolated locale seemed almost redundant. The limitations of the Pacific Northwest, and the depressed logging community in which he lived, hit him hard. He saw a future of soul-crushing anonymity, a lost artist in a lumberjack's body, and he decided that success as a musician was the only way out.

It was only a few years later that Kurt, by most measurements, achieved that goal. By the end of the 1980s, his indie band, Nirvana, had already developed a solid regional following. *Bleach*, the band's first album, was the top-selling jewel of the Seattle-based indie label Sub Pop Records. Kurt was a local alternative hero, but alternative was not what he was looking for. And while the image of Kurt Cobain as the disillusioned rock star has become something of a stereotype, it was the idea of *not* being a rock star that tortured him most. During his tenure at Sub Pop, he spent his off hours poring through books about the music industry, familiarizing himself with contracts, promotions, and distribution. "It's almost like he educated himself on how to be a rock star," one former Nirvana press rep told the journalist Everett True. In 1990, Sub Pop cofounder Bruce Pavitt heard rumors about his star pupils being whisked around town in limousines and wooed by major-label suits. Nirvana had signed with Sub Pop for a second album, but Kurt had other plans. He wanted to cut through the cheese of late-eighties radio with a new kind of pop music that was honest and edgy. After fielding offers from several major labels, Kurt and the other members decided on Geffen's DGC, the label with the strongest promotions department.

Nevermind, Nirvana's first DGC release, rose quickly to the top of the *Billboard* charts in 1992. With its concoction of buzz-saw guitars, angsty lyrics, and catchy hooks, the album bulldozed every last piece of bubblegum in its path, leaving record stores scrambling to figure out what to do with the crates of unsold Skid Row CDs. Through careful plotting, Kurt achieved his goal: Alternative was the new mainstream. Of course, the idea of a purposeful and driven Kurt

Cobain contradicts the reluctant rock star who once complained, "Famous is the last thing I wanted to be," but that statement was not entirely disingenuous. Famous is exactly what he wanted to be, if only to reclaim the euphoria of his predivorce childhood. But all the "voice of a generation" buzz in the world could not bring back that cozy feeling, and when success left him empty, he resented it. Moreover, he was becoming increasingly distraught over the symptoms of a painful stomach condition, for which he sought treatment for years only to leave doctors stumped. Kurt eventually decided that self-medication was his only option, and in the era of heroin chic— a few years before *Pulp Fiction* landed in theaters and Kate Moss on billboards—his medicinal choice was clear.

Nirvana was on top for only two short years before Kurt was found dead in his Seattle home of a self-inflicted gunshot wound. His suicide has since sparked a wave of conspiracy theorists who apparently have a hard time accepting the possibility that the composer of such songs as "Negative Creep" and "Rape Me" could have

Load Up on Puns

The direction of Nirvana's career—and popular music in general—changed forever with the release of "Smells Like Teen Spirit," which paved the way for the alternative-music maelstrom that dominated the airwaves until Hootie & the Blowfish brought blandness back to commercial radio. However, the song's amorphous title was actually just a misunderstanding. After a night of heavy drinking, Kurt's friend Kathleen Hanna, lead singer of the chick-punk band Bikini Kill, spray-painted "Kurt Smells Like Teen Spirit" on his bedroom wall. When Kurt saw the indoor graffiti the next morning, he thought it sounded bold, provocative—an acerbic critique on the unoriginality of an insipid youth culture. It wasn't until well after the song's release that Kurt learned the truth: Hanna was simply mocking the fact that he smelled like Teen Spirit antiperspirant, the brand of deodorant that his girlfriend wore at the time. Incidentally, the Mennen Company, which made the deodorant, was one of the primary beneficiaries of the song's success. Sales spiked after it became a hit, and the company was quick to capitalize on its popularity, even purposely airing a commercial spot before Nirvana's appearance on *Saturday Night Live*. Entertain us, indeed.

self-destructive leanings. However, it wouldn't have taken a coconspirator to predict such an outcome for Kurt Cobain, a tortured artist whose paradoxical attitudes toward celebrity and fame were probably best expressed on April 16, 1992, a few months after the explosion of *Nevermind*. Nirvana appeared on the cover of *Rolling Stone* magazine that week, with a rebellious Kurt donning a homemade T-shirt that declared "Corporate Magazines Still Suck." It was an act of defiance that could only have been topped by not appearing on the magazine in the first place. But that was never really an option. ∽

Vincent van Gogh
(1853–1890)

Abstract: Making the poster boy
Birth name: Vincent Willem van Gogh
Birthplace: Zundert, Netherlands
Masterwork: *Starry Night*
Demons: Mental illness

"It is absolutely certain that I shall never do important things."
—**Letter to the art critic J. J. Isaacson, 1890**

Throw out the term "tortured artist" in a game of Word Association and see how often "Vincent van Gogh" gets tossed back. The concept is as linked with the ill-kempt Dutch painter as "eccentric genius" with Albert Einstein or "supervillain" with Rupert Murdoch.

Yet we would know virtually nothing about van Gogh's torture if not for his brother Theo, a Paris-based art dealer who, shortly before his death from syphilis, asked his wife, Johanna, to seek recognition for the life's work of his late brother. At the time, Vincent was a relatively unknown painter who himself had died less than six months earlier from a self-inflicted gunshot wound, leaving behind hundreds of virtually worthless paintings.

Fortunately for Johanna, and for the insurmountable chore at hand, Theo also left something behind upon his death: a drawer full of letters that Vincent had written to him over the years—almost two decades' worth of correspondence. The letters chronicled Vincent's failed efforts to survive as an artist, following his travels through various cities in the Netherlands, Belgium, and France. But Vincent's writings revealed far more than a simple timeline of events. They also documented, in harrowing detail, the artist's steady progression of mental and physical anguish.

Collectively, the letters were a quasi-memoir of personal decline, weaving together a heartbreaking narrative of creativity, madness, and the relationship between the two.

On November 14, 1891, Johanna logged a diary entry about her plans to edit the letters for publication. "Before the summer rush begins, they have to be ready," she wrote. It would take her almost twenty-four years to complete that goal. During that time, largely through her own efforts in exhibiting Vincent's work, his reputation as a pioneering Post-Impressionist artist flourished throughout Europe. Growing almost as rapidly was the number of outlandish rumors about the artist's deeply troubled personal life, but in 1914, Johanna finally set the record straight and published *Letters to Theo*. For the first time since Vincent's untimely death, documented accounts of his torment were available for all to read.

> "the letters were a quasi-memoir of personal decline, weaving together a heartbreaking narrative of creativity, madness, and the relationship between the two"

So began the original story for tortured-artist mythology, with Vincent van Gogh emerging as both the archetype and stereotype for a new kind of antihero.

When today's tortured artists fall into trouble, they do so in front of the whole world. But at a time before cell phone cams caught our every misstep, *Letters to Theo* served as a companion piece for an artist whose reputation had long preceded him. And for early-twentieth-century voyeurs, intrigued by tales of the raving madman who cut off his ear, Vincent's detailed accounts enthralled and entertained. The letters confirmed, for instance, rumors of Vincent's compulsive and self-destructive behavior, as he wrote to Theo about his tendency to quiet his racing thoughts with cognac and absinthe. ("If the storm within gets too loud, I take a glass more to stun myself.") Conversely, Vincent's impassioned views on art, literature, and the creative process revealed complexities that far exceeded those of your average stumbling drunk. "God, how beautiful Shakespeare is," he wrote. "His language and method are like a brush trembling with excitement and ecstasy." And then there were endless descriptions of his frenzied but uneven creative output. Vincent could sometimes produce a painting a day, but he characterizes his frantic working pace as a mixed blessing—a symptom, he explains in the letters, of emotional highs and lows over which he had no control. One day he writes of feeling "twisted by enthusiasm . . . like a Greek oracle on the tripod." Another day, he expounds upon "horrible fits of anxiety, apparently without cause, or otherwise a feeling of emptiness and fatigue in the head."

And it only got worse. As Vincent entered his mid-thirties, the chasm between his boundless energy and crippling lethargy became more pronounced, ultimately leading to a downward spiral of depression, hallucinations, paranoid fits, and seizures. It was a seizure, in fact, that prompted the famous incident in which he lopped off a piece of his earlobe with a shaving knife. He had been drinking with his longtime friend, the artist Paul Gauguin, when the two got into an argument that ended with Vincent throwing a glass of absinthe in Paul's face. It was later that same evening that Vincent, in a throe of delirium, came after Paul with the razor blade before eventually turning the blade on himself. After the incident, Vincent was hospitalized, lapsing into a psychotic state that required three days of solitary confinement. Diagnosed with epilepsy, he was prescribed potassium bromide and was coherent within a few days after treatment.

But he didn't stay coherent for long. Around the time of his mental breakdown, Vincent's condition worsened when, in late 1888, he learned that his brother Theo was engaged to be married to Johanna Bogner. To Vincent, this was a threatening prospect. Theo was not only his closest friend and biggest fan but also his source of income, and Vincent was clearly worried about losing his brother's emotional and financial report. Soon after, Vincent entered a period that would be at once the most torturous and the most productive of his life.

By the spring of 1889, Vincent's delusions and hallucinations were routinely causing him to make a public spectacle of himself around Arles, France, where he was living. About thirty townspeople, fed up with the carryings on of the "red-headed madman," petitioned the local police to get rid of him. With nowhere else to go, Vincent entered the Saint-Paul Asylum in nearby Saint-Rémy. During the full year he remained there, he suffered at least three psychotic relapses, as well as prominent bouts of amnesia, but lest we picture the artist chewing on tubes of oil paint for twelve months, it's also important to point out his astounding productivity during this period. Although he grew increasingly frustrated by the fits, which kept him from painting, he also experienced pronounced stretches of clearheadedness and even ecstasy. He painted some 300 works at the asylum, including many of those for which he is most remembered. *Irises,* today among the world's most expensive paintings, shows a flower bed in the asylum garden. *Roses,* a favorite showpiece at the

Metropolitan Museum of Art, was painted just days before his release and left behind to dry. As for Vincent's swirly magnum opus, *Starry Night*, it depicts the view from inside his sanitarium room. Given that painting's enduring popularity, it's ironic that neither Vincent nor Theo was particularly happy with the work.

In the foreword for the 1914 edition of *Letters to Theo*, Johanna van Gogh-Bogner admitted the real reason that she waited almost a quarter century after Vincent's death before publishing the artist's correspondence in its entirety. It wasn't just the laborious process of editing the letters, she explained, but rather the desire to wait until his artwork had achieved its due acclaim. "It would have been unfair . . . to generate interest in his person before the work to which he gave his life was recognized and appreciated," she wrote. It's a fair point. After all, concerning ourselves with artists' lives before we know anything about their art reeks of the kind of cart-before-the-horse synthesis that favors Willow Smith over countless musicians slugging it out for exposure. A random Dutch painter as a tortured soul has little practical application in the absence of his vibrant blots of color and exaggerated lines—the techniques that gave birth to Expressionism and continue to have a huge influence over modern art to this day. Vincent van Gogh, like all great tortured artists, took his pain and twisted it around until it became the very thing he wanted most out of life. He suffered, but his suffering had a purpose. Maybe ours does, too. ∽

PART II

The Art

9

Tortured Artists Timeline

A Brief and Deliberately Random History of Pain, Suffering, and Artistic Triumphs

B.C.

25,000

Cave paintings emerge in Paleolithic Europe, depicting violent hunting scenes and other everyday horrors of prehistoric society.

3100

Written language develops in Mesopotamia only to be destroyed by Twitter nearly five millennia later.

1400

In Ancient Egypt, the most talented artists in the land are commissioned to paint elaborate depictions of Pharaonic life in the tombs of Luxor. Their talents are so appreciated that they are entombed—alive—when their benefactors die.

850

Homer writes *The Iliad,* an epic poem set during the Trojan War.

630

The Sapphic poet Sappho is born on the island of Lesbos. She later becomes the first female writer to break through the marble ceiling.

432

Phidias carves the Statue of Zeus, which becomes one of the seven wonders of the ancient world. Two years later, the artist is charged with embezzling gold and dies in prison.

335

Aristotle's *Poetics* marks the first comprehensive theory of literary and dramatic structures. Perhaps not coincidentally, literary and drama critics become annoying the following year.

29

Augustus Caesar bullies the poet Virgil into writing the *Aeneid,* a 10,000-line poem celebrating the glory of Rome.

A.D.

95

On the Greek Isle of Patmos, a cave dweller named John has a revelation about the end of the world. He writes the final chapter in what is arguably the most influential piece of literature in history: the Bible.

1048

Persian poet and unrepentant ladies' man Omar Khayyam is born in what is now Iran. Almost a millennium later, his *Rubaiyat* is quoted by another famous gadabout, President Clinton, as he apologizes to the nation for the Monica Lewinsky scandal.

1308

Hell-obsessed wordsmith Dante gives birth to the Italian language by standardizing a blend of southern dialects with Florentine and Latin (see Chapter 3).

1348

The Black Death wipes out roughly half the population of Europe, influencing art across the continent. Gothic allegories such as *Danse Macabre*, a morality tale about the universal nature of death, are all the rage.

1503

Leonardo da Vinci starts work on the *Mona Lisa*. The artist, a notorious procrastinator, labors over the painting for decades but never finishes it.

1564

William Shakespeare is born. His known body of work helps mold the English language into its modern form, leaving behind a sizable lexicon of great adjectives for tortured writers, including the word *tortured* itself.

1603

Japanese artists develop a new style of hyper-realist theater called *kabuki*. Pundits later refer to anything slightly over-the-top as "kabuki-esque."

A.D.

1606

Notorious bar brawler and king of chiaroscuro Caravaggio murders a "polite young man" over a tennis match. Pope Paul V issues a death warrant, but the lovely portrait of the pontiff that Caravaggio had painted earlier evidently plays well in the artist's favor, and he is soon pardoned.

1612

Artemesia Gentileschi, the first female painter to be accepted into the Accademia di Arte del Disegno, in Florence, is raped by her painting teacher. Afterward she makes a career out of painting decapitated men.

1631

Empress, muse, and world-renowned beauty Mumtaz Mahal dies. Her grief-stricken husband, Shah Jahan, commands the construction of an extravagant tomb for his beloved at her birthplace. Twenty years and 20,000 workers later, the Taj Mahal is finally finished.

1694–95

Johann Sebastian Bach is orphaned at the age of ten, when both of his parents die within eight months of each other. He moves in with his brother, who introduces him to music.

1750

Kikuya, a hot-footed shamisen player and part-time prostitute, becomes Japan's first professional female performing artist: a "geisha."

1774

The Sorrows of Young Werther, Goethe's semiautobiographical tale of an ill-fated love affair, inspires the earliest recorded instances of copycat suicide, as lovelorn young men around Germany kill themselves in the same manner as the book's tortured protagonist.

1791

Mozart dies while writing *Requiem* (see Chapter 1).

A.D.

1815–16

Troubled teen Mary Shelley pens her famous horror novel, *Frankenstein* (see Chapter 2).

1824

Unable to hear the audience's enraptured response to his Ninth Symphony, Ludwig van Beethoven is turned around by a contralto to see the noiseless clapping and cheers.

Charlotte Brontë is shipped off to the Clergy Daughters boarding school, where an abusive faculty and unsanitary living conditions serve as fodder for her signature novel, *Jane Eyre*.

1849

A semiconscious Edgar Allan Poe is discovered wandering around the streets of Baltimore (see Chapter 5).

1866

Emily Dickinson takes to wearing nothing but white dresses year round. Unfortunately, no one sees them, as she also becomes a recluse on her family's estate and will remain so until her death, twenty years later.

1873

When he isn't hiding turds under a friend's pillow, getting piss drunk on absinthe and stabbing his wrists, cussing out the town priest, or being shot in the arm by his lover, pretty-boy wordsmith Arthur Rimbaud finds time to write *A Season in Hell*.

1877

The final installment of Leo Tolstoy's *Anna Karenina* is released. In what is now known as the Werther Effect (see 1774), a suicidal memoirist named Sophia writes about leaping in front of an oncoming train as did the novel's heroine. Her estranged husband, Leo Tolstoy, is merely annoyed.

A.D.

1879

At fourteen, Henri de Toulouse-Lautrec breaks his second femur within eighteen months, permanently stunting both his legs while his torso continues to grow. He later makes a career of stripping the glamorous varnish from Parisian nightlife and exposing the ugliness of others.

1884

A three-year-old Pablo Picasso gets caught in an earthquake (see Chapter 1).

1889

Vincent van Gogh checks himself into the mental asylum where he will paint *Starry Night* (see Chapter 8).

1895

Oscar Wilde is convicted of "gross indecency." Devotees sport green carnations in their lapels, a secret Victorian symbol for fellow "sodomites" (see Chapter 5).

1900

Marcel Proust's lopsided scowl is immortalized in a photograph.

1902

An adolescent Irving Berlin runs away from home and starts singing for pennies in Bowery saloons (see Chapter 2).

1904

Arshile Gorky, a seminal figure in the American Abstract Expressionist movement, is born. His life will be beset with misfortune: His mother will die of starvation in his arms (after having survived the Armenian genocide); his studio will burn down; his wife will leave him; he will get cancer and wear a colostomy bag; he will break his neck, back, and painting arm in a car wreck; and then, at the age of forty-four, he will slash his last painting and hang himself from the rafters of a barn.

A.D.

1906

Vaudeville star and Gibson Girl Evelyn Nesbit's millionaire husband shoots and kills her lover, architect Stanford White. Alcoholism, morphine abuse, and serial suicide attempts take their toll on her beauty and career—both of which will quickly fade into oblivion.

1908

An eighteen-year-old Adolf Hitler is rejected by Vienna's Academy of Art. He gets a little bit upset.

1909

Screaming-pope painter Francis Bacon is born.

1910

Gustav Mahler seeks counsel from Sigmund Freud when he learns that his wife, the socialite and cultural strumpet Alma Mahler, is having an affair with Bauhaus founder Walter Gropius. Unable to shake his love for the cleft-chinned lovely, he dedicates his eighth (and most brooding) symphony to her.

1912

Egon Schiele is convicted of "public immorality" (see Chapter 5).

1915

D. W. Griffith's silent film *The Birth of a Nation,* based on the novel *The Clansman*, premieres. In later years, the film's leading lady, Lillian Gish, will claim to have been blacklisted from the entertainment industry due to accusations of anti-Semitism and right-wing xenophobia. Until her dying day, Gish will blindly defend the film's glaring racist content.

1917

At the age of ten, the future "Bronze Venus," Josephine Baker, witnesses the Race Riot of East St. Louis.

A.D.

1925

Theodor Geisel gets fired from the staff of his college magazine after he's caught drinking gin in his dorm. In order to keep contributing to the publication in secret, he starts going by his middle name, Seuss.

1926

Ingmar Bergman, the son of a sadistically authoritarian pastor, loses his faith at the age of eight. For the next six decades, he wrestles cinematically with religion—and his father's cruelty—most patently in his film that won four Academy Awards, *Fanny and Alexander.*

1927

Modern-dance pioneer Isadora Duncan's fondness for dancing with—and wearing—long, flowing scarves becomes her undoing when one wraps around the spoke of a convertible and snaps her neck. Gertrude Stein burps, "Affectations can be dangerous."

Fuddled flirt Clara Bow stars in *It* (see Chapter 1).

1929

Arthur Miller goes from riches to rags on Black Thursday, October 24 (see Chapter 2).

1931

Lee Strasberg, of New York's Group Theatre collective, develops Method acting. The technique encourages actors to get in touch with their inner pain, as if playing a dead hooker on *Law & Order* for twenty years isn't painful enough.

Todd Jones is born and develops a debilitating stutter that renders him virtually mute until high school. He will later lend his voice to one of the most shocking twists in blockbuster history when he booms, "Luke, I am your father." Long after giving up the nickname "Todd," James Earl Jones earns a new moniker: "The Voice of God."

1932

Cleveland high school student and aspiring artist Jerry Siegel is devastated after his father dies in a robbery. That same year, he teams up with his friend Joe Shuster to create a new character: a bulletproof avenger named Superman.

1934

Under Stalin's orders, Socialist Realism is officially defined by the Soviet Congress. The movement sweeps across the USSR, glorifying poor people in kitschy hyperrealistic fashion. Or else.

1938

Robert Johnson, the legendary blues guitarist and rumored soul seller, dies under mysterious circumstances. He becomes the founding member of the posthumous 27 Club.

1939

Growing bored with conventional jam sessions, Charlie Parker develops bebop, a complex style of improvisational jazz (see Chapter 7).

Jim Crow laws prevent Hattie McDaniel (who will become the first African-American Oscar winner) from properly attending the Atlanta premiere of *Gone with the Wind*. A descendant of slaves and a former maid herself, she was sometimes criticized for playing "the help," to which she responded, "I'd rather play a maid than be one."

1941

The United States enters World War II. The conflict provides American artists with endless content, from *Boogie Woogie Bugle Boy* to *Inglourious Basterds*.

1942

Abandoned by her husband, Foxy Sondheim takes out all of her anger and sexual frustration on her son, Stephen. The twelve-year-old seeks refuge with his friend's father Oscar Hammerstein, who schools him on how to weave the familial darkness into theatrical brilliance.

A.D.

1944

Jackson Pollock pees in Peggy Guggenheim's fireplace.

In August, Yves Montand and his girlfriend, Edith Piaf, lead an impassioned and defiant "La Marseillaise" at the Comedie-Francaise as American forces begin liberating France.

1945

Sarah Vaughan is denied entry into a whites-only hotel in Washington, D.C. Twenty years later she dances with President Johnson in the White House.

1948

Jack Kerouac coins the term "Beat Generation" in a landmark victory for hipster rights.

1949

George Orwell's dystopian novel *Nineteen Eighty-Four* eerily predicts state-sanctioned surveillance but glaringly omits cell phone cams.

1950

Peanuts, a comic strip by the broken-hearted cartoonist Charles M. Schulz, debuts (see Chapter 3).

1951

Little Brown & Co. publishes *The Catcher in the Rye* by J. D. Salinger. American teen angst is born.

1955

James Dean, the cinematic personification of teen angst, rebels without a cause—or a seat belt.

Black-clad Johnny Cash has his first hit with "Cry, Cry, Cry" (see Chapter 1).

A.D.

1956

A British tabloid accuses Liberace of being "fruit-flavoured," a term implying he was actually (wait for it) gay. The be-glittered, feathered, ermined, and jewel-encrusted Mr. Showmanship himself sues and wins. Once he receives the check for damages to the tune of £8,000, he sends a telegram to the reporter saying, "What you said hurt me very much. I cried all the way to the bank."

1957

Eugene O'Neill's *Long Day's Journey Into Night* wins the Pulitzer Prize for Drama. O'Neill, having died from alcoholism three years earlier, is unable to attend the ceremony.

1959

The monsignor of melancholy is born: Steven Patrick Morrissey, who will later be known strictly by his surname.

The French New Wave crests with François Truffaut's semiautobiographical tormented tale of childhood, *The 400 Blows*.

Ken Kesey, a writer and human guinea pig, volunteers to take part in a CIA-financed study on the effects of psychoactive drugs. His time at the mental hospital inspires his first published novel, *One Flew Over the Cuckoo's Nest*.

After being relegated to a tour bus, Waylon Jennings jokingly tells Buddy Holly, "I hope your ol' plane crashes."

1960

Federico Fellini's *La Dolce Vita* heralds the coming age of voyeurism and celebrity obsession through its protagonist, a sleazy tabloid photographer named Paparazzo. The term is derived from the Italian word for the buzzing sound of a mosquito.

After years of medical, legal, and financial troubles, Harlem Renaissance author Zora Neale Hurston is laid to rest in an unmarked grave in Florida.

A.D.

1961

The International Neo-Dadaist movement Fluxus flexes its nothingness. Five years later, pseudo-member Yoko Ono will break up the Beatles while Fluxus superstar and video artist Nam June Paik will encourage people to climb inside the vagina of a sperm whale.

1962

Marilyn Monroe dies at thirty-six (see Chapter 8).

1963

Sylvia Plath Hughes is laid to rest in Heptonstall, England. For decades her devoted acolytes will repeatedly chisel her married name off her headstone in patent smites against her pariah poet husband, Ted Hughes (see Chapter 8).

John Hughes goes to high school in suburban Illinois and never leaves (see Chapter 2).

1964

Lenny Bruce gets arrested for cursing at a Greenwich Village club (see Chapter 3).

1965

Recording what she intended as notes for her autobiography, Judy Garland admits, "I tried my damndest to believe in the rainbow that I tried to get over and couldn't. So what? Lots of people can't." (See Chapter 7.)

1966

Valerie Solanas hands her play *Up Your Ass* to Andy Warhol. Two years later, when he refuses to produce the charmingly titled work, she shoots him in the chest.

1969

John Kennedy Toole, depressed and humiliated by the rejection of his book *A Confederacy of Dunces,* hooks a garden hose to his car and gases himself to death. Twelve years later the novel will receive the Pulitzer Prize for Fiction.

1969—*continued*

With the Vietnam War at its peak, the Woodstock music festival calls for "three days of music and peace" among a generation of young, idealistic baby boomers—most of whom cut their hair and "get real jobs" within six months.

1970

More famous for her stints in asylums than soundstages, the actress Frances Farmer dies. Her volatile imbalance and striking beauty become the inspiration for three plays, a rock opera, a feature-length film, a made-for-TV biopic, and several books; even Kurt Cobain, Boy George, Everything But the Girl, and Mylène Farmer (who changed her name in Frances's honor) paid homage to Farmer in song.

Controversies and conspiracy theories swirl around the deaths of Jimi Hendrix in September, Janis Joplin in October, and Jim Morrison nine months later. All three were twenty-seven.

1971

Famed photographer and freak-fancier Diane Arbus takes a fistful of barbiturates, slits her wrists, and slips into a bathtub.

Shooting begins on *The Godfather*. Marlon Brando shows up for his paycheck and turns in one of the most memorable roles in film history (see Chapter 2).

1972

Though historians disagree on the exact hour, it is widely accepted that on the evening of October 5th, Elvis Aaron Presley transitioned to Fat Elvis.

1973

Reclusive janitor Henry Darger dies. His landlord, upon entering Darger's hovel, discovers a 15,000-page manuscript and hundreds of large cartoons depicting children involved in epic battles. Soon he will become an icon in the world of Outsider Art, and his paintings will fetch upward of $80,000.

A.D.

1973—*continued*

Carly Simon's "You're So Vain" tops the charts. Thirty-seven years later, Warren Beatty is devastated to learn that the song was not entirely about him—rather it was inspired by an apricot-scarfed David Geffen.

Hilly Kristal opens CBGB on the Bowery, where he intends to showcase country, bluegrass, and blues acts. The club becomes the birthplace of punk within a few months (see Chapter 6).

1974

Seven-year-old Kurt Cobain is prescribed Ritalin for Attention Deficit Disorder (see Chapter 8).

1975

Karen Carpenter's battle with anorexia nervosa brings the disorder to the collective forefront when the Carpenters are forced to cancel their Japanese and European tours. With her body too damaged to fully recover, she dies eight years later at the age of thirty-two.

1977

Diane Keaton wins an Oscar for her portrayal of Annie Hall, a character Woody Allen created after getting dumped by Diane Keaton.

1978

Artist Robert Mapplethorpe shoves a bullwhip up his ass and takes a picture.

1979

Michael Jackson undergoes his first plastic surgery at the age of twenty-one. It seems harmless at the time (see Chapter 1).

1980

Pink Floyd's *The Wall*, a concept album about the depths of human isolation, tops the *Billboard* 200. Grammar geeks debate whether the double negative in the line "We don't need no education" is meant to be ironic.

A.D.

1980—*continued*

Richard Pryor freebases cocaine, ignites himself with 151-proof rum, and runs down the street. Two years later, after much psychological and physical rehabilitation, he will joke about it to thunderous guffaws.

Love tears Ian Curtis apart.

Annie Leibovitz shoots a naked John Lennon wrapped around his wife. Five hours later, Lennon is shot again—this time on the sidewalk in front of the Dakota.

1981

Christina Crawford's tortured childhood tale, *Mommie Dearest,* makes it to the big screen, defying any critic with fingers to not type some variation of the word "kabuki" (see 1603) in their reviews.

1982

John Belushi parties for the last time at the Chateau Marmont (see Chapter 7).

1983

Tennessee Williams dies in what looks like a set of one of his own plays—a chic New York hotel suite littered with half-empty wine bottles and pills peppered about the room.

1984

Dr. Haing Somnang Ngor, himself a survivor of the Khmer Rouge, becomes the first Asian actor to win the Academy Award, for his debut performance in *The Killing Fields.* Twelve years later, he is shot dead in the Chinatown section of Los Angeles—rumored under orders from Pol Pot.

1986

Ice-T propels gangsta rap into the mainstream with the single "6 in the Mornin'." Its realistic depiction of inner-city violence among African-American youths speaks to white suburbia.

A.D.

1987

Matt Groening, an obscure cartoonist for the alt-weekly *Los Angeles Reader*, uses his own dysfunctional family as a model for the Simpsons.

1988

The ancient Romans may have invented graffiti, but it was Jean-Michel Basquiat who brought it from the streets to the most important museums the world over. His prolific career is cut short, however, when he dies at the age of twenty-seven of a heroin overdose.

1990

French artist Orlan begins cosmetic procedures that will give her the features of famous works of art (the chin of Botticelli's *Venus*, for instance) but ends up looking like Mr. Potato Head and scaring the living hell out of innocent children.

1991

The all-girl punk band Bikini Kill publishes the Riot Grrrl Manifesto.

Disturbed and disturbing photographer Guy Bourdin dies—but not until his wife and two girlfriends kill themselves first.

1992

Sinéad O'Connor, protesting the tyranny of the Catholic church, tears up a photograph of Pope John Paul II on *Saturday Night Live*. Nothing compares, however, to the sound of one million eyes rolling.

1993

Actor River Phoenix overdoses on heroin and cocaine outside the Viper Room in the early morning hours of Halloween.

1995

Actor Iron Eyes Cody, after a lifetime of playing Algonquians, Cherokees, and chiefs—and most notably for his portrayal of the "Crying Indian" in one of the most effective PSAs ever—is finally honored by Hollywood's American Indian community for his contribution to the representations of Native American life.

A.D.

1996

Iron Eyes Cody is given something to really cry about when he is exposed as an Italian American, born Espera Oscar de Corti to Sicilian immigrants.

Jonathan Larson's *Rent* debuts on Broadway, providing an explosive soundtrack for Alphabet City grit just in time for gentrification. Larson died earlier that year on the day before its off-Broadway premiere.

Like her aunt, uncle, and grandfathers before her, Margaux Hemingway continues the family tradition and offs herself—on the day before the anniversary of her grandfather Ernest's suicide.

1999

Dana Plato dies of a drug overdose almost two decades after the first airing of *Diff'rent Strokes.*

2000

Edward Albee writes *The Goat, or Who Is Silvia?,* a play about the love that dare not bleat its name.

2001

One week after the September 11 terrorist attacks, Eric Fischl finishes his bronze sculpture *Woman Tumbling* in response to people leaping to their deaths from the World Trade Center. The piece will be exhibited eight years later, though quickly covered up due to protests.

In an effort to pay off his enormous drug rehabilitation bills, the former child star and *Teen Beat* cover boy Corey Haim attempts to sell one of his teeth on eBay.

Actor Dennis Hopper has the first retrospective of his artwork at Amsterdam's Stedelijk Museum. He acknowledges his indebtedness to Pollock, Warhol, and Rauschenberg—as well as years of heavy drug and alcohol abuse.

A.D.

2002

Andrew Bujalski's *Funny Ha Ha* launches the mumblecore film movement. Ultra-low-budget directors, disillusioned with the Hollywood studio system, finally have a voice, albeit an inaudible one.

Nicole Kidman slaps on a plastic nose and takes home an Oscar for portraying one of the most tortured writers of all time, Virginia Woolf.

2003

Nina Simone, the High Priestess of Soul, who once shot a teenager just for interrupting her concentration, dies at her home in the south of France.

2004

In January, after a lifetime of suffering from clinical depression, actor and playwright Spalding Gray jumps from the Staten Island Ferry. Two months later his body is recovered from the East River.

2006

Boy George apparently wanted to hurt himself when he called police about a phony burglary and then got busted with thirteen bags of cocaine.

2007

To prepare for the role of the Joker in *The Dark Knight*, Heath Ledger locks himself in a hotel room (see Chapter 7).

2008

Amy Winehouse punches a fan (see Chapter 7).

2010

Lee Siegel, a critic for *The New York Observer*, declares, "Fiction has become culturally irrelevant." His comment evokes outrage among the dozen or so people who still read *The New York Observer*.

Godmother of Performance Art Marina Abramović has a 736.5-hour staring contest.

2011

Andres Serrano, after twenty years of staunchly defending his infamous photograph of a crucifix submerged in urine, titled "Piss Christ," learns that the piece has been destroyed by protesters in France.

Elizabeth Taylor dies. Debbie Reynolds (whose husband dumped her for the violet-eyed beauty) laughs, "Elizabeth loved life, and I know; she took part of mine."

New York's legendary Hotel Chelsea, former hothouse/flophouse to countless artists and writers—and site of an alleged murder by Sid Vicious—closes its doors to guests and goes condo.

Appendix: Source List

Introduction

ALFRED HITCHCOCK

Chandler, Charlotte. *It's Only a Movie: Alfred Hitchcock: A Personal Biography*. New York: Applause, 2006.

Chapter 1

PABLO PICASSO

Gómez, Pedro Luis. "Picasso: Childhood of a Genius." *SUR in English: The Newspaper for Southern Spain*, February 21–February 27, 2003.

McGowen, Tom. *Space Race: The Mission, the Men, the Moon*. Berkeley Heights, NJ: Enslow Publishers, 2009.

Miller, Alice. *The Untouched Key*. Translated by Hildegarde and Hunter Hannum. New York: Anchor, 1991.

Richardson, John. *A Life of Picasso: The Prodigy, 1881–1906*. With the collaboration of Marilyn McCully. New York: Knopf, 2007.

CLARA BOW

Stenn, David. *Clara Bow: Runnin' Wild*. Lanham, MD: Cooper Square Press, 2000.

St. Johns, Adela Rogers. "Clara Bow: My Life Story." *Motion Picture Classic Magazine*, July 1928.

JOHNNY CASH

Cash, Johnny. *Johnny Cash: The Autobiography*. With Patrick Carr. New York: Harper Paperbacks, 1998.

Streissguth, Michael. *Johnny Cash: The Biography*. Cambridge, MA: Da Capo Press, 2006.

ANDY WARHOL

Bockris, Victor. *Warhol: The Biography*. Cambridge, MA: Da Capo Press, 1997.

Koestenbaum, Wayne. *Andy Warhol*. New York: Viking, 2001.

Scherman, Tony, and David Dalton. *Pop: The Genius of Andy Warhol*. New York: HarperCollins, 2009.

MICHAEL JACKSON

Jones, Jel D. Lewis. *Michael Jackson, the King of Pop*. Phoenix: Amber Books, 2005.

Taraborrelli, Randy J. *Michael Jackson: The Magic and the Madness*. New York: Birch Lane Press, 1991.

WOLFGANG AMADEUS MOZART

Gutman, Robert W. *Mozart: A Cultural Biography*. Boston: Mariner Books, 2000.

Karhausen, Lucien R. "Mozart's 140 Causes of Death and 27 Mental Disorders." *British Medical Journal*, November 2010.

Solomon, Maynard. *Mozart: A Life*. New York: HarperPerennial, 1996.

Chapter 2

MARY SHELLEY

Seymour, Miranda. *Mary Shelley*. New York: Grove Press, 2000.

Tambora Volcano, Indonesia. U.S. Geological Survey. *http://vulcan.wr.usgs.gov/Volcanoes/Indonesia/description_tambora_1815_eruption.html*.

IRVING BERLIN

Bergreen, Laurence. *As Thousands Cheer: The Life of Irving Berlin*. Cambridge, MA: Da Capo Press, 1996.

Burton, Jack. "The Honor Roll of Popular Songwriters." *Billboard*, May 28, 1949.

ARTHUR MILLER

Gottfried, Martin. *Arthur Miller: His Life and Work*. Cambridge, MA: Da Capo Press, 2003.

Lamos, Mark. "An Interview with Arthur Miller." *Michigan Quarterly Review*, April 2004.

MARLON BRANDO

Bosworth, Patricia. *Marlon Brando*. New York: Viking Adult, 2001.

Kanfer, Stefan. *Somebody: The Reckless Life and Remarkable Career of Marlon Brando*. New York: Knopf, 2008.

JOHN HUGHES

Carter, Bill. "Him Alone." *The New York Times*, August 4, 1991.

Gora, Susannah. *You Couldn't Ignore Me If You Tried*. New York: Three Rivers Press, 2011.

Kamp, David. "Sweet Bard of Youth." *Vanity Fair*, March 2010.

Chapter 3

DANTE

Alighieri, Dante. *La Vita Nuova*. Translated by Barbara Reynolds. Baltimore: Penguin Classics, 1969.

Bondanella, Peter. "Introduction and Notes." In Dante Alighieri, *The Inferno*. Translated by Henry Wadsworth Longfellow. New York: Barnes & Noble Classics, 2003.

JANE AUSTEN

Spence, Jon. *Becoming Jane Austen*. London: Hambledon Continuum, 2003.

Walker, Linda Robinson. "Jane Austen and Tom Lefroy: Stories." *Persuasions On-Line*, a publication of the Jane Austen Society, 27:1 (Winter 2006).

W. B. YEATS

Arkins, Brian. *Builders of My Soul: Greek and Roman Themes in Yeats*. Lanham, MD: Rowman & Littlefield, 1991.

Cahill, Christopher. "Second Puberty." *The Atlantic Monthly*, December 2003.

Smith, Stan. *W. B. Yeats: A Critical Introduction*. New York: Palgrave Macmillan 1990.

CHARLES M. SCHULZ

Johnson, Rheta Grimsley. *Good Grief: The Story of Charles M. Schulz*. Kansas City, MO: Andrews McMeel, 1995.

Michaelis, David. *Schulz and Peanuts*. New York: Harper, 2007.

LENNY BRUCE

Bruce, Lenny. *How to Talk Dirty and Influence People*. Chicago: Playboy, 1963.

Goldman, Albert. *Ladies and Gentlemen—Lenny Bruce!!* From the journalism of Lawrence Schiller. New York: Penguin, 1992.

Wiede, Robert B. *Lenny Bruce: Swear to Tell the Truth*. HBO Documentary, 1998.

Chapter 4

MICHELANGELO

Jones, Jonathan. *The Lost Battles: Leonardo, Michelangelo and the Artistic Duel That Defined the Renaissance*. London: Simon & Schuster, 2010.

Rolland, Romain. *The Extraordinary Life of Michelangelo (Illustrated)*. Translated by Frederick Street. Edited by Shawn Conners. El Paso: Special Edition Books, 2010.

Srinivasan, Archana. *World Famous Artists*. Chennai, Tamil Nadu, India: Sura Books, 2004.

MARIA CALLAS

De Carvalho, George. "The Prima Donna." *Time*, October 29, 1956.

McMahon, Barbara. "Revealed: Callas's Secret Passion for Recipes She Refused to Taste." *Guardian*, July 24, 2005.

Petsalis-Diomidis, Nicholas. *The Unknown Callas: The Greek Years*. Portland, OR: Amadeus Press, 2001.

WALT DISNEY

Gabler, Neal. *Walt Disney: The Triumph of the American Imagination*. New York: Random House, 2006.

Famous Quotes from 100 Great People. Boston: MobileReference, 2011.

MADONNA

Ciccone, Christopher. *Life with My Sister Madonna*. With Wendy Leigh. New York: Gallery, 2008.

Cross, Mary. *Madonna: A Biography*. Westport, CT: Greenwood Press, 2007.

Skow, John. "Show Business: Madonna Rocks the Land." *Time*, May 27, 1985.

J. K. ROWLING

Brown, Jonathan. "In Memory of Her Mother, J K Rowling's £10M for MS." *The Independent*, September 1, 2010.

Dunn, Elisabeth. "From the Dole to Hollywood." *The Telegraph*, June 30, 2007.

Greig, Geordie. "There Would Be So Much to Tell Her." *The Telegraph*, January 10, 2006.

Winfrey, Oprah. "The Brilliant Mind Behind *Harry Potter*." Interview of J. K. Rowling on *The Oprah Winfrey Show*, October 1, 2010. *www.oprah.com/oprahshow/ The-Brilliant-Mind-Behind-Harry-Potter*.

JAMES CAMERON

Boucher, Geoff. "James Cameron: I Want to Compete with 'Star Wars' and Tolkien." *Los Angeles Times*, August 26, 2010.

Davis, Joshua. "James Cameron's New 3-D Epic Could Change Film Forever." *Wired Magazine*, December 2009.

Smith, Krista. "James Cameron: The *Vanity Fair* Interview." *Vanity Fair*, December 2009.

Chapter 5

EDGAR ALLAN POE

The Edgar Allan Poe Society of Baltimore. www.eapoe.org.

Meltzer, Milton. *Edgar Allan Poe: A Biography*. Minneapolis: Twenty-First Century, 2003.

Silverman, Kenneth. *Edgar A. Poe: Mournful and Never-Ending Remembrance*. New York: Harper Perennial, 1992.

OSCAR WILDE

Holland, Merlin. *The Real Trial of Oscar Wilde*. New York: Harper Perennial, 2004.

McKenna, Neil. *The Secret Life of Oscar Wilde*. New York: Basic Books, 2005.

Wilde, Oscar. *De Profundis*. North Charleston, SC: CreateSpace, 2011.

EGON SCHIELE

Fernandes, Andréa. "The 'Enfant Terrible' of Austria: Egon Schiele." *Mental Floss* blog, June 16, 2009. *www.mentalfloss.com/blogs/archives/26485*.

Hamilton, Adrian. "Egon Schiele—The Man Who Loved Women." *The Independent*, May 23, 2011.

Jones, Jonathan. "The Come-On." *Guardian*, April 19, 2003.

Owen, Catherine. *Somatic: The Life and Work of Egon Schiele*. Toronto: Exile Editions, 1998.

H. G. WELLS

Mackenzie, Norman and Jeanne. *H. G. Wells: A Biography*. New York: Simon & Schuster, 1973.

Wells, H. G. *The Fate of Man*. New York: Alliance, 1939.

DOROTHY PARKER

Day, Barry. *Dorothy Parker: In Her Own Words*. Lanham, MD: Taylor Trade, 2004.

Meade, Marion. *Dorothy Parker: What Fresh Hell Is This?* New York: Penguin, 1989.

CHUCK BERRY
Junod, Tom. "What I've Learned: Chuck Berry." *Esquire*, December 31, 2001.

Peg, Bruce. *Brown Eyed Handsome Man*. New York: Routledge, 2002.

Poore, Billy. *Rockabilly: A Forty-Year Journey*. Milwaukee: Hal Leonard Corporation, 1998.

Chapter 6

GILBERT AND SULLIVAN
Jones, John Bush. *Our Musicals, Ourselves*. Hanover, NH: Brandeis University Press, 2003.

Mayer, Bernard S. *Staying with Conflict*. San Francisco: Jossey-Bass, 2009.

Oost, Regina B. *Gilbert and Sullivan: Class and the Savoy Tradition, 1875–1896*. Farnham, England: Ashgate, 2009.

LUCILLE BALL AND DESI ARNAZ
Ball, Lucille. *Love, Lucy*. New York: Putnam, 1996.

Sanders, Coyne S., and Tom Gilbert. *Desilu: The Story of Lucille Ball and Desi Arnaz*. New York: It Books, 2011.

JOEY AND JOHNNY RAMONE
Leigh, Mickey. *I Slept with Joey Ramone*. With Legs McNeil. New York: Touchstone, 2009.

Spitz, Marc. "The Last Testament of Johnny Ramone." *Spin*, November 2004.

IKE AND TINA TURNER

Alexander, Amy. *50 Black Women Who Changed America*. New York: Citadel, 1999.

Cohen, Scott. "The Legacy of Tina Turner." *Spin*, January 1990.

Creeden, Sharon. *In Full Bloom: Tales of Women in Their Prime*. Atlanta: August House, 1999.

Winfrey, Oprah. "Oprah Talks to Tina Turner." *O, The Oprah Magazine*, May 2005.

WERNER HERZOG AND KLAUS KINSKI

Herzog, Werner. *Herzog on Herzog*. Edited by Paul Cronin. New York: Faber & Faber, 2003.

Winter, Jessica. *The Rough Guide to Film*. London: Rough Guides, 2007.

Chapter 7

JUDY GARLAND

Alexander, Shana. "Judy's New Rainbow." *LIFE Magazine*, June 2, 1961.

Clarke, Gerald. *Get Happy: The Life of Judy Garland*. New York: Delta, 2001.

CHARLIE PARKER

Cooke, Mervyn, and David Horn, eds. *The Cambridge Companion to Jazz*. Cambridge: Cambridge University Press, 2002.

Filan, Kenaz. *The Power of Poppy*. Rochester, VT: Park Street Press, 2011.

Woideck, Carl. *Charlie Parker: His Life and Music*. Ann Arbor: University of Michigan Press, 1996.

JOHN BELUSHI

Belushi-Pisano, Judith, and Colby Tanner. *Belushi: A Biography*. New York: Rugged Land, 2005.

Shales, Tom, and James Andrew Miller. *Live From New York: An Uncensored History of Saturday Night Live as Told By Its Stars, Writers, and Guests*. Boston: Back Bay Books, 2003.

Thomas, Mike. *The Second City Unscripted*. New York: Villard Books, 2009.

Woodward, Bob. *Wired: The Short Life & Fast Times of John Belushi*. New York: Pocket, 1989.

HEATH LEDGER

Biskind, Peter. "The Last of Heath." *Vanity Fair*, August 2009.

Giles, Jeff. "Young Wonder from Down Under." *Newsweek*, July 10, 2000.

Helling, Steve. "Heath Ledger's Last Days." *People*, June 29, 2009.

Lyall, Sarah. "In Stetson or Wig, He's Hard to Pin Down." *The New York Times*, November 4, 2007.

Maher, Kevin. "Heath Ledger: The Accidental Hero." *The Times*, October 14, 2006.

AMY WINEHOUSE

Eliscu, Jenny. "The Diva and Her Demons." *Rolling Stone*, June 14, 2007.

Frere-Jones, Sasha. "Amy's Circus." *The New Yorker*, March 3, 2008.

Kandell, Steve. "Everyone's Talking About This Crazy Bird Amy Winehouse . . . Except Amy Winehouse." *Spin*, July 2007.

Willman, Chris. "A Labour of Love." *Entertainment Weekly*. May 18, 2007.

Chapter 8

MARILYN MONROE

Churchwell, Sarah. *The Many Lives of Marilyn Monroe*. New York: Picador, 2004.

Erickson, Steve. "Blonde of the Century." *Los Angeles Magazine*, June 1, 2001.

Meryman, Richard. "Marilyn Monroe Lets Her Hair Down about Being Famous." *LIFE Magazine*, August 3, 1962.

Taraborrelli, J. Randy. *The Secret Life of Marilyn Monroe*. New York: Grand Central Publishing, 2009.

SYLVIA PLATH

Plath, Sylvia. *The Bell Jar*. New York: Harper Perennial Modern Classics, 2006.

Plath, Sylvia. *The Journals of Sylvia Plath*. New York: Ballantine Books, 1987.

Stevenson, Anne. *Bitter Fame: A Life of Sylvia Plath*. New York: Mariner Books, 1998.

KURT COBAIN

Azerrad, Michael. *Come as You Are: The Story of Nirvana*. New York: Broadway Books, 1993.

Cameron, Keith. "Nirvana." *Sounds*, October 1990.

Cross, Charles R. *Heavier Than Heaven*. New York: Hyperion, 2001.

"Smells Like the Imaginative Media Buy of the Month." *Adweek*, January 20, 1992.

VINCENT VAN GOGH

Blumer, Dietrich. "The Illness of Vincent van Gogh." *The American Journal of Psychiatry* 159 (April 2002): 519–526.

Meier-Graefe, Julius. *Vincent van Gogh: A Biography*. Mineola, NY: Dover Publications, 1987.

Thompson, Richard. *Vincent van Gogh: The Starry Night*. New York: The Museum of Modern Art, 2008.

The Vincent van Gogh Gallery. "The Letters." David Brooks. *www.vggallery.com*.

Other Resources

Centers for Disease Control and Prevention. Adolescent and School Health. "Youth Risk Behavior Survey Fact Sheets." *www.cdc.gov/healthyyouth/yrbs/factsheets/index.htm*.

Erickson, Paula. "Billboard & Nielsen SoundScan List Taylor Swift as the Top-Selling and Most-Played Artist of 2010." Erickson Public Relations Press Release, January 7, 2011. *www.reuters.com/article/2011/01/07/idUS166394+07-Jan-2011+PRN20110107*.

Hingley, Ronald. *A New Life of Anton Chekhov*. New York: Knopf, 1976.

Jamison, Kay Redfield. "Manic-Depressive Illness and Creativity." *Scientific American*, 1995.

Ludwig, Arnold. *The Price of Greatness*. New York: Guilford Press, 1995.

Meloy, J. R., and H. Fisher. "Some Thoughts on the Neurobiology of Stalking." *Journal of Forensic Sciences* 50(6) (2005 Nov): 1472–80. Abstract online at PubMed.gov. *www.ncbi.nlm.nih .gov/pubmed/16382848*.

Radner, Gilda. *It's Always Something*. New York: Simon & Schuster, 1989.

Rojas, Carlos. *Salvador Dalí, or The Art of Spitting on Your Mother's Portrait*. University Park: Pennsylvania State University Press, 1993.

Rothenberg, Albert. *Creativity and Madness*. Baltimore: The Johns Hopkins University Press, 1994.

Index

Acknowledgments

First and foremost, I am indebted to my agent, Meg Thompson, who believed in this idea from the beginning and whose disarming use of the word "bummer" in the face of several setbacks kept me from reaching for the nearest bottle of Prozac. I am also cheerfully grateful for my editor at Adams Media, Brendan O'Neill, who instantly took to the idea that all artists are tortured, regardless of when and where they are born and what type of art they practice. Ditto to my development editor, Jennifer Lawler.

Of course, I could not have ducked out of the office long enough to write this book had it not been for the leniency of my boss at *Show Business* magazine, David Pearlstein. Thanks also to several colleagues past and present: John Rowell, Doug Strassler, Nicole Steen, Lucy Butcher, Elise McMullen, Karen Greco, Amy Krivohlavek, Ethan Kanfer, Andrea Meek, and Julie Colthorpe. Special thanks to James Taylor for his design ideas, and, of course, Robbie Lee for his illustrations.

Christina D'Angelo, whose vast repository of arts knowledge puts mine promptly to shame, was indispensable in her writing, research, and constant supply of fresh ideas. Also, several intelligent yet artsy people looked at early drafts of the tortured artists timeline and offered great suggestions: Kailee Ayyar, Aurora Celepija, Angela Di Carlo, Peter L. Goldman, Vladimir Janev, Elizabeth Katusa, Caroline Rush, Merrie Nell Spence, Stephanie Smith Wilkins, Kristin Villanueva, and I'm pretty sure most of the staff at I Trulli Ristorante. I also received invaluable feedback from my wonderful parents, Joseph and Elizabeth, and my endlessly creative brothers, Joe and Fred.

Finally, it goes without saying that this book would not have been possible without the brilliant and meticulous research of countless biographers and journalists, who have spent God knows how many hours uncovering the compelling narratives hidden within the life stories of so many great artists. Thank you for your terrific work.

About the Author

Christopher Zara is a writer, critic, and journalist who writes about pop culture, entertainment, and the arts. He is the managing editor of *Show Business* magazine, a trade publication for the performing arts industry. Christopher's work has appeared in such magazines as *Mental Floss, MovieMaker, Dramatics, Stage Directions,* and *Emmy.* He lives in New York City. His website is *www.christopherzara.com.*

About the Illustrator

Robbie Lee is an artist and art teacher who has been drawing and painting professionally for more than twelve years. He designs T-shirts through commissions at such websites as TeeFury, Threadless, and Design By Humans. He lives in Orlando, Florida. His website is *www.robbielee-illustrator.com.*